No One
Listened

No One Listened

Two children. A horrific act of violence.
No one to trust except each other.

ISOBEL AND ALEX KERR

with Andrew Crofts

In loving memory of our Mum

HarperElement
An Imprint of HarperCollins*Publishers*
77–85 Fulham Palace Road,
Hammersmith, London W6 8JB

The web address is www.thorsonselement.com

and *HarperElement* are trademarks
of HarperCollins*Publishers* Ltd

First published by HarperCollins*Publishers* 2008

1

Copyright © 2008 Isobel and Alex Kerr

Isobel and Alex Kerr assert the moral right to
be identified as the authors of this work

A catalogue record for this book
is available from the British Library

ISBN-10 0-00-727245-6 (hardback)
ISBN-13 978-00-727245-7 (hardback)
ISBN-10 0-00-727246-4 (paperback)
ISBN-13 978-00-727246-4 (paperback)

Printed and bound in Great Britain by
Clays Ltd, St Ives plc

Chapter One

Alex

Normally my sister Isobel would have got home from school before me, but that afternoon she'd been held up because she couldn't find her PE kit in the changing rooms and she and a friend had stayed behind to look for it. I'd been let out of class a few minutes earlier than usual and I'd walked straight home, just as I always did. If Isobel had left at her normal time and got home before me, she would have let herself into the house before the police arrived to stop her and she would have seen everything. Maybe he would even have attacked her as well.

The day it all happened was the 11th of January, 2002. It was a little after three-thirty in the afternoon so it was already on the verge of growing dark as I crossed the busy main road that ran between our home and our school. I was thirteen and Isobel was fifteen and we had been walking to and from school on our own for a good few years by then. There was nothing unusual about the journey, nothing to alert me to the waiting danger or to the horror of what had just happened behind our locked front door. I was thinking about normal, routine things like the homework I had to do and the after-school activities planned for that evening, and I was wondering what was for dinner.

The first thing I noticed as I came into our quiet road was that Mum's red Vauxhall Nova was parked outside the house. She wouldn't normally have got home from her job as a school teacher for a couple of hours yet and she hadn't said anything about being early when she set off that morning, so that puzzled me.

I turned into our front garden and walked the few paces up to the house, then pulled out my front door key, just as I always did, without even thinking about it, ready to let myself in. As I lifted the key to the lock, a movement in the street behind made me turn and I saw a police car drawing up at the kerb, its vivid markings making it stand out amongst all the other parked cars. I paused for a second and watched as a young uniformed policeman, dressed in a bullet-proof vest and looking a bit like one of those SWAT teams you see breaking into people's houses in television dramas, got out of the driver's door. There didn't seem to be any great sense of urgency in his movements so I turned back to the door and inserted my key in the lock. The policeman called out, making me jump.

'No, no lad,' he shouted. 'Stop there. Don't go in. Wait over there a minute.'

He walked up behind me and nodded towards the low wall that separated our front garden from next door's. There wasn't anything particularly dramatic in his tone as he gave me those instructions; it all seemed a routine matter to him, although I found it odd that I was being stopped from going into my own house. Isobel and I had always been brought up to be respectful of authority figures so I did as he told me without question, leaving my key still in the lock, unable to work out what was going on and unsure what to ask. It's always been my habit to stay quiet in new situations where I am unsure of myself, and wait to see what happens rather than launch in with lots of questions, demanding to know what was going on, which is probably what Isobel would have done if she had been in my shoes at that moment.

Under my curious gaze the policeman composed himself and then politely rang the doorbell, as if he was just paying a visit. I wondered if perhaps Mum and Dad had been arguing again and neighbours had rung to complain about the noise or to express their concern for Mum's safety. I decided I wasn't going to interfere, in case it was Dad who came to the door; I would leave it to the policeman to sort it out.

Dad had often threatened to hang himself or set fire to the house with us all in it. It might sound melodramatic but I believed anything was possible as far as he was concerned. Maybe this time he had actually carried out one of his threats and Mum had had to call the police. Isobel and I were so worried about his threats to set fire to us that before we went to bed at night we used to try to find all the matches in the house and hide them – which was pointless really as we had no idea what Dad kept inside his room. We had never been allowed inside the upstairs bedroom where he spent most of his days and nights; we didn't even have any idea what it looked like in there.

A few seconds after the policeman rang the bell, the door opened and Dad was standing there, holding it wide open and giving the officer a clear view right through to the kitchen at the back of the house. I was over to the side so I couldn't see past them. Dad didn't seem at all surprised to find a uniformed policeman standing on his doorstep; it was as if he had been expecting him. He's a big guy, quite scary-looking, with a mean expression permanently set on his face. Whatever the policeman was able to see from there was enough to make him step back in shock and fumble for his radio, bringing it up to his mouth.

'There's been a blue murder,' he announced to whoever might be listening at the other end.

I was momentarily puzzled by the phrase. 'Screaming blue murder' just meant screaming at the top of your voice, as far as I was aware, but maybe this was police code for something else – or had I not heard him correctly? The policeman certainly looked very shaken and it was more because of his agitation than anything else that I guessed someone was dead in the house. My throat felt tight, but I continued to sit where he had told me, not saying a word, just watching and waiting, trying to work out what was going on and what I should do about it. That was how I reacted to most things. The policeman seemed to have forgotten I was there, or at least he didn't look in my direction. He stepped back from the door and peered anxiously down the road.

For a few minutes nothing happened and then the eerie quiet of the afternoon was shattered by screeching tyres and brakes as another squad car arrived and disgorged four more officers. I could hear further vehicles arriving behind them, stopping wherever they could, filling the street. Now there was a real sense of urgency buzzing all around me as I sat on the wall and waited for someone to tell me what I should do. I kept wondering where Mum was, but at the same time not wanting to think about the possible answer to that question. Please no.

Dad was still standing in the doorway as if he had been expecting the police all along and he didn't protest as one of the policemen read him his rights. 'You do not have to say anything. But it may harm your defence if you do not mention when questioned something which you later rely on in court.' Dad didn't struggle as they searched him; he raised his arms to let them pat down his jeans and t-shirt top. They removed a knife from his jeans pocket, handling it carefully as if it was something precious.

'Can I say something to my son?' Dad asked them, glancing over towards me for the first time.

'You should have thought of that before,' the senior officer said and I was quite relieved. I couldn't imagine that I would want to hear anything he might have to say to me at that stage. I never wanted to hear anything he said, in fact. It felt good to have the protection of the policemen, but I just wished I understood why they were swarming all over us now when they had never done anything to help us before, on any of the occasions when Isobel had called them because Dad was being violent.

I watched from the wall as they led Dad out of the house. Several policemen formed a kind of ring around me and I got the impression that they thought I might try to go with him, but they needn't have worried; I wasn't intending to go anywhere, certainly not with Dad. They led him to the second police car and bent him down so he could slide into the back seat. I watched as the shiny bald crown of his head disappeared inside. By that stage seven more police cars had arrived, as well as five unmarked cars, two ambulances and a paramedic car. It was hard to imagine where they could all have come from to get there so quickly. Had they just been sitting around waiting for something to do? The whole street was jammed solid with vehicles.

None of the police said anything to me, all of them apparently too busy trying to work out what they should be doing. I was just waiting for Isobel to get there because she would know what we should do; she would talk to them and find out what was going on. I could always rely on Isobel. Where on earth was she? A few minutes later, I was filled with relief when I saw her familiar figure turning into the road.

Chapter Two

Isobel

The greatest mystery is why Mum and Dad ever got together in the first place because Alex and I never saw the slightest sign of any bond of affection or attraction between them. Even when couples have been worn down by years of money worries, job worries and family worries, you can usually see some remnants of the love that must once have been there – but not with our Mum and Dad. You could see that Mum wanted to please him, but only because she was frightened of what he would do if she didn't, and because she wanted a quiet life more than anything else. He, on the other hand, could never hide his loathing of her for even a second and took great pleasure in making her life as difficult as possible.

If there was any sort of romance or love story in their background, neither of them ever mentioned it to Alex or me, and there's no one else we can ask because there are no other family members who knew them when they were young. Our family was never very good at talking about emotions or soul-searching. We all just got on with the business of daily life, pushing unpleasant thoughts to the backs of our minds in the hope they would go away if we ignored them for long enough.

The only source of information we have about the past is Jillian, who was Mum's good friend at the school where she taught for twenty-three years, and one of the very few people to whom she ever confided any of those sorts of secrets. Mum didn't believe in sharing personal information with anyone unless she had to. She kept everything locked inside her head, probably trying to forget most of it herself. Several teaching colleagues who had known her for twenty years or more didn't even realise she was married, although they knew all about Alex and me and our achievements. She wouldn't have encouraged conversations about her marriage and there certainly wasn't anything nice she could say about Dad. I know she wouldn't have wanted to let anyone else know that her personal life was a horrible nightmare.

As far as we could see, Mum and Dad were totally unsuited to one another, and Dad was totally unsuited to family life in any form at all. He should probably never have married and he should certainly never have had children. Of course we didn't realise that when we were young; we assumed lots of fathers behaved the way he did. Our friends' dads were at work most of the time so we didn't have much contact with them; our social world was largely made up of other children and their mothers, so the fact that our Dad remained locked inside his bedroom most of the time didn't seem particularly odd to start with. It was just the way things were done in our house.

We do know that when Mum and Dad first met, her parents weren't at all happy about the match. Maybe that was part of the attraction for Mum – her one and only act of rebellion against Granddad, who was the big authority figure in her life. She had come from a very disciplined background and it may be she wanted to prove to my grandfather, who was in the military police, that she could make her own decisions, that she wasn't going to be under his thumb all her life. If that is the case, it was a very bad decision and one she must have regretted bitterly. But once Mum had made a commitment to something there was no way she would ever go back on it. She had agreed to marry Dad and to stay with him 'for better and for worse', and she never for a second wavered from that path even though the places it led her were always 'worse' and never 'better'. Maybe she just wanted to have children and Dad was the first person to propose to her. I'll never know now.

Nan and Granddad lived in a bungalow in Torquay and we would go with Mum to visit them every half term and during the holidays, but Dad never came with us. They wanted nothing to do with him and I imagine he wanted nothing to do with them either. There must have been something about him right from the beginning that made it obvious he wouldn't make a good husband for Mum, or for anyone come to that. Neither Granddad nor Nan ever said anything about him in front of us; in fact I don't remember his name ever being mentioned in their company. As far as they were concerned, it was as if he didn't exist.

Even once he'd retired from the army, Granddad was still incredibly strict and humourless, constantly barking out orders and finding fault with everything we did, as if he was inspecting us on the parade ground. By the time we knew him he was already an old man who spent most of his time sitting in a chair puffing on his pipe and glowering at us if we made a sound, but it was easy to imagine how fierce he must have been with Mum when she was young. We were never allowed to play when he was around; we had to sit still and keep quiet. We could only have fun if we went out somewhere with Mum and Nan, or played outside with the other kids in the area with whom we had made friends during our visits. Alex and I were always quite good at making friends in new places, never troubled with shyness.

Granddad didn't seem to care much for any of us, and Alex and I certainly didn't like him. Maybe he was disappointed with the way Mum's life had turned out, but he didn't seem to make any effort to improve things for her, apart from letting us come to stay with him in the holidays. If he was as irritated by our invasion of his peace and quiet as he seemed to be then I suppose that was a sacrifice we should be grateful to him for making.

Nan was Mum's stepmother. Her real mother had died very young, while Mum was still a teenager, but as far as Alex and I were concerned Granddad's wife was our real grandma; she was the only one we ever knew and no one told us that our real grandma was dead until we were much older. It was another of those things that wasn't talked about. Our family was full of secrets like that; things that were just never mentioned because they were felt to be too personal and private or possibly even too painful. Alex and I knew instinctively not to ask questions, that Mum didn't want to talk about any personal things. None of it really mattered to us as long as she was around anyway. Children only really care about their own little worlds and because she took care of everything in our lives we never had any reason to delve into the shadows of our family history.

By the time we were old enough to want to understand more about the past, it was too late because Mum and Nan and Granddad were all dead. As long as we were small we didn't have to question why anything was how it was because Mum made sure everything worked out okay. We knew her world revolved around us and that she would do anything for us, so there was no need for soul searching, no need to try to poke our noses into corners of our family business that she obviously preferred to ignore. We had enough to occupy and stimulate our minds as it was. Children are usually happy to accept life at face value as long as they feel secure and loved and know where they stand. We always knew exactly where we stood with Mum.

I was about ten when Granddad died, and Alex was seven. Nan moved to King's Lynn and died not long afterwards herself. It must have been a blow to Mum despite her difficult relationship with her father, because the trips to Torquay had been an escape for her and us, allowing us to get away from Dad and all the problems at home. Although Granddad was a joyless man, he was still a lot nicer to her than Dad, and Nan was always sweet and friendly. Apart from anything else they had provided us with holiday accommodation and there was no way Mum could afford to take us away so often once we didn't have somewhere free to stay.

I think Dad's family background must have been very different to Mum's, although we never met anyone who knew anything about him or his childhood. It was almost as though he had arrived in our house fully formed as a reclusive middle-aged man, with no history and no past that was ever spoken about. Mum never talked about him and we certainly wouldn't have asked him any direct questions. We knew a few basic facts, and we found out a few more at his trial, but nothing that actually shed any light on how he became the man we knew.

He was from the north-east, Newcastle I think, born in 1948, and we have been told he was one of a family of twelve, but we have never met his parents or any of his brothers or sisters so we have no way of knowing if that is true. Even when one of his brothers came to work in Redditch, the town south of Birmingham where we lived at the time, we still didn't get to meet him. I don't know if he and Dad saw each other then, but Dad would never have introduced him to us anyway. He liked to keep each part of his life secret and separate from every other part, as if that gave him some sort of illusion of control. He hated Mum and me, for reasons I have never fully understood, so why would he want to introduce us to his brother? He probably hated his brother as well, although I never remember him even mentioning him. He hated pretty much everyone, except Alex.

Every so often Mum would say something that gave us the tiniest glimpse into the past, but we were too young to find out more. I know that Dad had already been in trouble with the law by the time he met Mum, although I'm not sure what for. I believe he had run away from home and had spent some time in borstal for stealing. He always claimed that that spell in borstal was 'the best time of his life', as if he was remembering happy

no one listened

school days. I can imagine that was true, because he never liked having responsibility for anything, or taking decisions, or looking after himself. Being locked up in an institution that took care of every decision for him would have suited him perfectly. He was never any good at dealing with money or paying bills or any of the mundane chores that the outside world demands of you. So although we never knew the details of the crime he had committed to be locked up in such a place, we got the impression he was a bit of a tearaway from the start. That certainly wouldn't have appealed to a disciplined and authoritative military man like Granddad.

Dad said a few things at his trial about how hard his childhood had been, claiming that was why he was the way he was, but the judge didn't seem to take any notice. Nothing that could have happened to him as a child in the nineteen-fifties could justify what he did that afternoon in January 2002.

I suspect that even as a girl Mum was always bright and hard-working. I expect she was eager to please Granddad to begin with and that he put pressure on her to do her best at school. She went to university a little bit later than most people, when she was already well into her twenties. She never told us what happened in those intervening years, but once she was set on her life's course to graduate and become a science teacher, nothing would distract or deter her.

She went from her home in Manchester to university in London and it was while she was there that she met Dad, who had come down from Newcastle around the same time to work as a computer repairman. Maybe they found they had common ground because both of them had escaped from their families and were living alone in a big, strange city. Maybe because she was a bit older than most of the other students on her course she didn't have many friends in the university, and Dad was almost certainly a bit of a loner himself. Whatever the reasons, they moved in together in Finsbury Park, north London, and embarked on their doomed relationship.

Once she had her degree Mum went to work in a school in Wolverhampton and they got married in 1979. They bought a house in Redditch, a town about an hour's drive from Wolverhampton. I've no idea how they came to choose Redditch and why they didn't live nearer to the school where Mum worked, but they were still there when I was born in 1986. I never questioned it because that was just the way things were. All our lives the routine was the same, with Alex and me going to school locally, Mum commuting to Wolverhampton and Dad locked inside his bedroom in the house. The hour's commute meant Mum had to get up early every morning in order to drive herself to work for the start of school, but she would always be back in time to take Alex and me to our evening activities, and she was always there with us during the school holidays. So, apart from her not being around to get us to school in the mornings, she was there for us whenever we wanted her and we had no reason to want things to be any different. Small children are very accepting of the status quo as long as they feel loved and cared for. However bad our parents' relationship was, we had no reason to feel insecure ourselves.

All the driving Mum had to do at the beginning and end of each working day must have been horribly tiring for her, although she never complained about it. She hardly ever complained about anything when we were young, never discussed anything to do with emotions or feelings, just got on with the practical matters of life in the most efficient way possible. It was only as we got into our teens that the strain began to show, the exhaustion wearing away her patience more and more frequently. If we had only known about the pressure she was under during those years we might have taken more care of her, but she never told us anything, just soldiered grimly on.

She definitely enjoyed her work, maybe because she knew she was good at it and had the respect of all her colleagues. We didn't really think about what she might be like as a teacher, but I remember that she always seemed to know everything about her pupils – about their hopes and ambitions and the progress they made towards realising them. She seemed to take a genuine interest and to have their best interests at heart almost as much as she had ours.

We went to her school a few times when there was some special event, like a piano exam we had to attend, and it always seemed to me to have a pretty tough atmosphere. I remember sitting outside her classroom once, hearing the pupils kicking off and making a noise in a way we would never have done at our school. She did say once or twice she wouldn't want to live in Wolverhampton, even though it would be more convenient for travelling, because she would always be bumping into kids in the town centre and they were more than likely to be shouting abuse. I suppose that sort of behaviour happens in most schools but Alex and I never came across it in our own school because we were always in the top sets for everything, where kids tend to be more motivated to learn and better behaved as a result.

Mum was already head of the science department by the time I was aware of what she did for a living, and her friend Jillian was her personal laboratory technician. She didn't talk to us about events at the school much, but I remember the skin on her hands had become stained and thickened over the years from constant contact with a variety of chemicals. It grew so thick eventually that she was able to lift baking trays and casseroles in and out of ovens without even feeling the heat. Her appearance never concerned her; she was too busy all the time rushing to get on with whatever she had to do next, whether it was driving us somewhere, shopping or marking school work, to even think about it. She had a short, easy-to-keep haircut and wore smart, practical skirts and blouses with low-heeled shoes for work. I don't ever remember her dressing up for an evening out; she wasn't the dressy type.

Mum was already working with Jillian and her other colleagues at the time Alex and I were born, so she had been talking to them about us all our lives. They knew all about us even though we knew nothing about them. Her office was covered in pictures of us, and we were never in any doubt how much she loved us and how proud she was of our achievements; it just felt strange to think of her talking about us to virtual strangers.

She can't have talked much to anyone about Dad because they didn't seem to know anything about him. Jillian told us later that Mum had tried inviting a few of her closest work friends back home for supper when she first joined the school, before I was born, but Dad obviously hadn't been keen.

'Once we were all there,' she told me, 'he came walking into the room completely naked. Your poor mother didn't know what to say. It was as if he was doing everything in his power to make us feel uncomfortable and threatened, to make sure that Mum would never ask us or anyone else back.'

19

I guess he was trying to demonstrate that his house was his private kingdom and that he resented the fact he had to share it with Mum, let alone with complete strangers. He probably felt threatened by the thought of a bunch of teachers talking about the sort of things that interested them, and felt as if he was being deliberately excluded in some way. He wanted to keep Mum all to himself. He was happy enough for her to go out and earn money to keep him but he didn't want her working life encroaching on his territory. Mum must have got the message pretty quickly because she stopped inviting people to the house after that – not that any of them were likely to want to come back once they had experienced the full weirdness of being in a confined space with Dad. We were used to his oddities, like leaving all the doors and windows open in mid-winter, or threatening to hang himself, or walking round naked, or leaving rude messages for Mum on the white board that hung in the kitchen, but other people found it quite intimidating.

Some women would have realised at that early stage that they had made a mistake in their choice of husband and would have got themselves out of the relationship as quickly as they could, but Mum had made a commit-ment and she was going to stick to it, however hard Dad might make it for her.

They got married in a registry office and from the few photographs that survive it doesn't look as though any of their families or friends attended the ceremony. The only other people pictured apart from the happy couple themselves are their two witnesses, neither of whom we recognise. It's possible they were strangers brought in off the street to make the process legal. It seems that Dad had already cut himself off completely from his family by then and that Granddad was not willing to relent in his disapproval of the match, not even on the wedding day itself. It must have been sad for Mum that it was such a low-key affair but, knowing Dad, it probably suited him right down to the ground.

By going through with a marriage to a man her father hated, Mum had shown that she was willing and able to stand up to him. I imagine in most cases where the parents disapprove of their children's choice of partner, they relent and put a brave face on it during the actual wedding day, but it doesn't look as if anyone in our family was willing to climb down from their high horse and compromise. For Mum it must have seemed like a bleak start to their married life, but maybe she convinced herself that she liked it, that it was her choice too, that she 'didn't want any fuss'. That would have been entirely in character.

She looks happy in those early photos, quite normal really. Dad looks a bit of a sinister presence in the background, wearing a black suit and shades, but maybe that's just with the benefit of hindsight. Maybe because we know how disturbed and dangerous he later became we assume the signs were all there to start with. It's strange for us looking at old pictures of him before he lost his hair and before he started to bulk up and become heavy-looking. To the casual glance they look like a normal young couple starting out on life's journey together.

When they moved to Redditch and bought the house, they put it into their joint names. With that simple and normal marital action, Mum entrapped herself still further. To escape from Dad after that would have meant giving up her home as well as her marriage, an option that became impossible for her to countenance once she had one, and then two children.

Our home was a very normal, three-bedroom, semi-detached Victorian house with an extraordinarily long garden behind it, just like a million others up and down the country – but most of them house perfectly normal, happy families. No one walking past on the quiet street outside and glancing up at our windows would have been able to imagine that there was anything sinister or out of the ordinary developing behind its façade.

Mum didn't have me until she was thirty-five. I don't know why she waited so long or why she finally decided to start a family then, when there must already have been problems in their relationship. Maybe she wanted to get to a certain point in her career first, or maybe she got pregnant by mistake, or maybe she was trying to get pregnant all those years and it just took a long time. We never talked about such personal matters with her, so now we will never know. Whatever the reasons, from the moment Alex and I arrived in the world she was completely focused and dedicated to guiding us to fulfil every ounce of potential we might possess. Perhaps that was when the cracks in the marriage really started to show, when Dad no longer had her undivided attention and he realised he was going to have to share her with two demanding little newcomers.

There are pictures of Dad holding me as a baby and smiling. It seems unbelievable to me that such a scene could ever have happened because I have no memory of a time when he didn't hate me and Mum. In fact by the end he hated almost everyone to some degree. We didn't know the full extent of it until his trial, but even before Alex and I were born Dad was creating trouble in the street and getting a reputation with the neighbours for being a nightmare. There were times when he would wander into people's gardens uninvited and move everything around, digging up and replanting flowers and bushes. No one could work out whether he thought he was being helpful to his neighbours or if he was deliberately trying to annoy them. Few liked to challenge him because he was a frightening-looking man – tall, aggressive and unkempt, with a mean face. Most normal people were intimidated by him. He didn't care what anyone thought of him, but he wanted them to know just how much he hated them. He had a citizen's band radio fitted into his van and he connected it to loudspeakers and drove up and down the street shouting and swearing, broadcasting his views to the world, like a foul-mouthed politician on some bizarre mutation of an election battle bus. He had big bull bars fitted to the front so that he could push and bully his way into parking spaces, making everyone hate him even more. He was anti-social in every possible way.

He particularly terrorised the old lady next door to us, shooting water pistols at her through the fence when she was out in her garden and shouting abuse at her. One night her garage caught fire in mysterious circumstances and the fire brigade had to be called to extinguish it. To my amazement Alex didn't even wake up amidst the clamour of bells and shouting. The fire officers said the fire had definitely been started deliberately but there was no proof it was Dad so nobody had the nerve to accuse him to his face.

There was a family living opposite us whom Mum, Alex and I became very friendly with, despite Dad's antics. Mum asked the couple, Helen and Steve, to be our godparents when we were baptised. They had four children ranging from our age upwards and were a normal happy family, so we always liked going over there to

24

visit. For the first fifteen or so years of my life we all grew up together and I know Mum looked on them as the people she would have wanted us to go to if anything happened to her and Dad, since we had no close relatives. In fact, she told us so on several occasions. Their kids went to the same school as us, and did many of the same after-school activities, so Mum and Helen spent a lot of time together, often combining resources and driving one another's children along with their own. I think Mum confided more to Helen than she did to anyone else in our neighbourhood, although I never overheard them talking about anything very personal.

I was friendly with one of their daughters, who was roughly the same age as me, and when we were young she came to our house for tea a few times. She even stayed to have a bath with me once, but Dad liked to bath us at that stage and my friend didn't feel comfortable with that, which was hardly surprising. She didn't come round much after that occasion, which was fine with me because it meant I got to go to her house instead or to play outside more. Any excuse to get out of the house and away from Dad's silent, scowling presence was always welcome. Even when he was locked in his room we could sense his malevolence all over the house, all of us waiting nervously for him to emerge unexpectedly some-where, shouting at us to get out of his sight.

Chapter Three

Alex

Idon't think Dad can ever have been committed to the idea of working for a living, even though he did have a job when he met Mum. We had no idea at the time but at his trial we discovered that as far back as the 1970s he was already having trouble getting on with other people at work, always picking fights, arguing and threatening to leave. He never seemed able to get on with anyone. It was as if he had been meant to be a recluse from the moment he was born.

I guess he had no choice but to join the world of work when he first left Newcastle because he had to support himself somehow, but once he was married and Mum was earning a steady living from teaching, it became possible for him to start withdrawing from life outside the house.

When Isobel was born Mum had every intention of continuing to work because she loved her job and because she already knew that she couldn't rely on Dad to earn enough to keep a family. She had never been the sort of woman who would have been happy to stay at home, cooking and cleaning and waiting for her man and her children to return each evening. Maybe that was one of the reasons she had chosen to marry Dad, because she knew he would never ask that of her, that he would be happy for her to pursue a career, if only to get the house to himself for most of the day and to have money coming in without having to work for it himself.

Initially, when they were both working, Mum was prepared to pay for babysitters and childminders to take care of Isobel while they were out during the day, but it wasn't long before Dad realised that he could use his baby daughter as an excuse to give up work and stay home all the time. Maybe he genuinely thought that he could be a full-time 'house husband'.

Although Mum realised he had no interest whatsoever in looking after the baby, at least he would be there in the house with Isobel, so Mum thought she could go out first thing in the morning knowing that the baby had an adult in charge of her. Even then she must have suspected he wasn't at all the right man for the job, but he was Isobel's father so why shouldn't he be given the chance to look after her? Perhaps at that stage they were still kidding themselves that they were a normal married couple with a family, making normal, rational decisions about how to organise their lives in the most efficient way. Or maybe Mum just didn't think she had any option.

It wasn't long before she realised her mistake. She would come home after a long day at work to discover that Isobel was still exactly where she had left her that morning. Nappies weren't changed, she hadn't been fed, and it was obvious to her that Dad had basically taken no notice of the baby at all. He might have told her that he had given up work with the intention of caring for his first child, but it soon began to dawn on her that he wasn't capable of it. Within a few days Mum had to go back to hiring babysitters just as she had first intended. Dad, however, had got used to the idea of not working by that stage and made no effort to look for another job beyond the odd temporary one when he was in desperate need of cash for something. As Mum rushed around trying to earn enough to pay for his upkeep as well as Isobel's, and then mine, Dad withdrew further and further into his own private world, most of which was contained behind the closed doors of his silent bedroom, unseen by anyone but him.

'It's like having a third child to look after,' Mum would grumble on the rare occasions when she said anything about him at all. It certainly can't have felt as though she had a partner to share her life and her children with.

His inner sanctum had been Mum's bedroom as well when they first bought the house, but by the time Isobel and I were old enough to take in what was happening at night we realised that Mum always slept on the couch in the sitting room. During the day her pillow and duvet would be tucked away behind it, out of sight, and she would make up the bed last thing each night when she was ready to sleep. Her few clothes and possessions were kept in Isobel's room, so that she never had to invade Dad's privacy or risk waking him while he slept the days away.

'It's because I snore, and because I have to get up early,' she would explain if either of us questioned her about it. 'I don't want to disturb your father.'

We didn't question this logic; we just took it as normal. She made no complaint about the situation so we assumed it was okay and she was happy about it. Dad's bedroom became a mysterious world hidden behind a permanently closed door. Half the time when we came back from school we didn't even know if he was inside or not. Because he led such a nocturnal life there would often be no sounds emitting from behind the door during the day at all. He came down to the kitchen to make meals while we were out at school and never ate with the three of us. We knew he had a television in his room but we could never hear it, so I don't know if he ever actually watched it. Not knowing if he was in the house at any given moment made living under the same roof as him all the more scary.

We tried to carry on with our lives as if he didn't live there at all but sometimes he would suddenly appear on the landing or in the kitchen, usually saying nothing and staring straight through us. He had a habit of coming out of the bathroom stark naked and standing at the toilet with the door wide open, as if he didn't know anyone else was there. If we heard him coming in time we would dodge out of his way so we didn't risk incurring his wrath, but unless he deliberately wanted to pick a fight he wouldn't give any indication that he had seen us or that he even knew we existed. Isobel and I would have our showers before leaving for school in the morning, when we could be pretty certain he was fast asleep and wouldn't be disturbed by any noise we might make.

If he did speak to Isobel it was only to tell her how much he hated her. When she was little she didn't reply, but she grew bolder in later years and would sometimes even insult him as long as there were other people around to protect her if necessary. I remember she once told him he was 'gay', just to wind him up. It sometimes seemed as if she was deliberately courting danger, wanting to goad him into doing something terrible. If she had known just how deeply disturbed and dangerous he must have been through all those years, she would probably have been more careful. We all would have acted differently if we had had any idea we were living with a ticking time bomb. But you don't realise these things when you are too close to them, too used to them.

no one listened

Our main babysitter in the early years was a kind hippyish lady called Rita, who had long grey hair. Once we were both enrolled at school, Rita would take us in after Mum had left for work and get us to school on time, then pick us up in the afternoon at the end of lessons. We would go back to her house to play until Mum got back from work in Wolverhampton and collected us. Rita was perfectly nice and it didn't bother me that Mum wasn't there because I always had my big sister with me. I didn't want to go back to our house when Dad was the only grown-up there. There was no way of predicting what sort of mood he would be in, even though he always favoured me over Mum and Isobel.

He really hated them and it was as if he was trying to recruit me onto his side in the psychological war he insisted on waging against them. As a small boy I liked the attention when he was being nice to me, but I could never be confident he wouldn't shout at me or do something crazy like opening all the doors and windows in the middle of winter, or egging me on to do something wrong then telling Mum it was all my fault. Life was altogether safer and more predictable round at Rita's house, so I didn't complain. I wasn't the sort of child to complain about things anyway. There was no doubting how dedicated Mum was to Isobel and me.

As we got older and harder to entertain, Rita used to take us back to our own house after school rather than her own. Most days Dad's bedroom door would be closed when we came in and we would have no idea if he was in the house or not. It didn't worry us as long as the door remained closed, because we were used to living our lives without him. Isobel was still at lower school, so she would have been about seven when Rita stopped escorting us to school in the mornings and Mum told us we were old enough to go back and forth alone as long as we were together. I suppose she needed to save as much money as possible since she was supporting the family on one teaching salary. It wasn't that far to walk but we did have to cross the main road, which was pretty scary, and I would hold on tightly to Isobel's hand. From then on, my sister looked after me pretty much all the time that Mum was at work. Even though she was only two years older than me it seemed to come very naturally to her. She hardly ever complained about it because we got on so easily together. I was pretty stubborn about things I felt strongly about, but I wasn't one to argue or throw tantrums or make her life difficult unnecessarily. We didn't have much time for anything like that anyway, because there was always so much to do from the moment we woke up to the moment we fell back to sleep.

Isobel and I would usually be woken up by the sound of Mum going out the front door at seven-thirty in the morning. It would then be our job to take our mongrel, Alfie, out for a walk before we left, so that he would be able to hold on till we got back. We all knew Dad wouldn't be willing to get up and take him out during the day. If anything made Alfie bark, it would drive Dad completely mad.

Sometimes when we got up Isobel and I would come downstairs and find that Mum had overslept and was still curled up on the sofa, completely laid out with exhaustion and we would have to wake her so she could dash out to work.

We have quite a lot of photographs from our child-hood, but hardly any of Mum – probably because she was the one holding the camera. Dad would never have agreed to take photographs of her. There are one or two pictures in the old family albums of Dad playing with us when we were young. He looks quite happy and normal in them, but it can't have happened that often because I have no memory of him doing anything nice with us. I think there used to be more pictures of him but he ripped them up during one of his rampages, when he was thumping around shouting: 'I don't want to have anything to do with any of you!'

He destroyed a lot of the pictures of Isobel, too, because he hated her so much. 'She looks too much like your mother,' he told me, as if that was explanation enough.

There are still a lot of snaps that have survived despite his worst efforts, so Mum must have been very handy with the camera. It's more evidence of how proud she was of us and how important we were to her, which was probably why we were able to put up with Dad's lack of love relatively stoically. He wasn't able to undermine our feelings of self-worth because Mum had done such a good job of building them up in the first place.

There's one snap of us all on a beach together, like a normal family, but we don't know where that could be because neither Isobel or I can remember him ever coming on holiday with us. He built a climbing frame for us in the garden too, so there must have been moments when he did the right thing, but such moments became rarer as time passed and life made him more angry.

I was about seven when Granddad died, meaning that we couldn't go to Torquay on holiday any more. Mum still took us to Devon or Cornwall in the summer holidays, but there was never any question of Dad coming along. We certainly wouldn't have wanted him to. We used to spend our time bike riding, swimming in the sea and trying every activity we could find. All of us liked to be busy and stimulated; we were never ones for sitting around and relaxing, whereas Dad did nothing else. When it was just the three of us together we always got on well, all interested in doing the same sorts of things. I nearly always got sunburned because I'm pale-skinned and we were spending virtually all the daylight hours outdoors.

Granddad didn't leave any money to Mum in his will, which she was very hurt about at the time. I expect he wanted to keep his money out of Dad's clutches, so he put it in a trust set up so that Isobel and I and Nan's grandchildren would each receive a few thousand pounds when we turned eighteen. All Mum inherited was his old car, which I think she thought was a bit unfair. It was probably very wise of Granddad considering what happened in the end.

When Dad eventually took against me as well, he would often deny that I was his son, accusing Mum of having had an affair. It was a ridiculous accusation because Mum was the least likely person ever to do such a thing and because I looked just like him. In fact, by then I would have been quite pleased to have found out that I wasn't anything to do with him. He had an unlimited appetite for unpleasantness. He would make things up just to provoke a fight and to give himself an excuse to be vile to Mum or Isobel, and later on to me as well. In the early days he wanted me to join in with him in everything, even his drinking. I can remember the first time he made me drink whisky when I was about eight or nine, but I hated the taste so much I wouldn't take more than a few sips. It was as if he was trying to mould me into being more like him and less like Mum and Isobel, goading me on to be a bit of a rebel.

no one listened

When I was little he liked to take me out into the garage with him while he was fiddling with the cars, making out that we were doing it together although in reality I was just sitting there watching him most of the time. I think he was more interested in separating me from Mum in order to annoy her than in actually trying to teach me anything useful.

I was on my own with him in the house the day he had a stroke. I was just six years old and Mum had taken Isobel to her karate lesson. Dad and I had been messing about with the car in the garage. We came back into the house and as he started to walk upstairs he suddenly collapsed and crashed back down onto the hall floor. I don't think I panicked; I just went over to shake him and call to him, thinking he had fallen asleep. When I found I couldn't rouse him, I sat down on top of him to wait until Mum and Isobel got back. I wasn't particularly scared. I was confident that Mum would know what to do. She always did.

Chapter Four

Isobel

When Mum and I got home on the day of Dad's stroke, she put her key in the lock as usual and pushed the door, but it immediately hit an obstacle, refusing to open wide enough to let us in. Peering through the gap we could see Dad lying across the hall-way where he had fallen down the stairs, motionless. Alex was sitting on top of him, waiting patiently, as he always did for everything.

'Dad's asleep,' he told us, solemnly.

'We'll come in the back,' Mum told him and we hurried round the house to let ourselves in through the kitchen.

Mum knew immediately that Dad wasn't asleep and an ambulance must have been called, although I don't remember it arriving. I do remember going to visit him in hospital later, as he recovered. It wasn't until many years afterwards that we discovered that Mum had told our godmother, Helen, that she had hoped he would die that day. She called Helen to come over before she dialled 999 and apparently said she was considering not calling an ambulance for a while, in the hope that he would just slip peacefully away. It would have been a merciful release for all of us if that had happened, but Mum would never actually have been able to do such a thing, however miserable he was making her life by then. If he had died that day maybe we would still have Mum with us today. Things must already have been very bad between them for her to be thinking such terrible thoughts about him. Not all strokes are fatal, though, so we'll never know if it would have done much harm to have left him on the hall floor a bit longer.

He recovered almost completely over the coming months, although his movement never came back completely because he refused to have the physiotherapy that the doctors recommended. He wouldn't have wanted to put himself in someone else's power like that. He needed to be separate from the world and having someone manipulating him physically would probably have felt too personal. He hardly ever spoke to us so it was hard to tell if his speech had been affected, as it can be after a stroke; as far as I'm aware it didn't seem any different.

Once he was back home Dad's stroke made no differ-ence to any of our lives. Mum went back to work, we went back to school and he went back into his bedroom as if nothing had changed. But who knows what pressure the condition was putting on his brain, both before and after it happened? Did he act the way he later did because of the stroke, or did he have a stroke partly because of the stress he put himself under by hating the whole world?

All Mum's efforts were channelled into giving Alex and me the best possible start in life, and she refused to accept that anything was ever important enough to disrupt the relentless and steady routine of our educational and after-school activities. Feeling a bit ill, for instance, was never an excuse for missing anything. We actually had to be at death's door before she would let us use illness as an excuse to stay home or go to bed. Maybe she was fearful that we might have enough of Dad's genetic make-up to make us give up on life if she didn't keep us continually encouraged and stimulated. If that's the case I don't think she needed to worry, because neither of us wanted to be in the least like him.

Dad took no interest in any of Mum's plans for us. In fact he took no interest in us at all, apart from hating me and trying to recruit Alex to his cause of annoying Mum as much as possible. He would seize any chance he could to upset me. Knowing that I was terrified of dogs, for instance, he brought home a mongrel puppy, which we christened Alfie. He was a lovely dog, black with gold-coloured paws and eyebrows. Dad told Alex in advance what he was planning to do, which delighted Alex because he'd always wanted a dog of his own. The plan backfired on Dad because Alfie was so endearing I immediately overcame my fear and loved him as fiercely as Alex did, while having a dog in the house nearly drove Dad mad, particularly when Alfie barked and forced him to come out of his room unnecessarily. He grew to hate Alfie just as much as he hated us and he would lash out and kick or beat him so often the dog became a quivering mass of nerves whenever Dad was around – which annoyed him even more.

I had other pets over the years, which gave Dad more opportunities to get at me. There was the pet rabbit that he let out of the cage and chased away, taking pleasure in telling me that it would never survive in the wild. And there was the hamster he poisoned and cut open, leaving the corpse for Alex and me to find when we got back from school. It lay in the cage, looking as if it had been turned inside out with all its internal organs on display, and I retched at the sight, knowing straight away who must be responsible. If there was anything that I really liked, Dad would destroy it just for the pleasure of making me unhappy. I began to grow a protective layer over my emotions, always expecting the worst and never letting his cruelty get to me in the way he hoped. Even though he couldn't stand it when either of us cried, he still liked to try to make us, just to prove he could. The deaths of the pets was probably more upsetting for Alex, because he was that bit younger than me, but Dad was willing to pay that price.

Bit by bit he taught me that I could never trust him, never hope that he would change or do something nice for me, and I learned to hide my emotions from him at all costs so that he wouldn't be able to see when he got to me. But the less I reacted to his campaigns of hate, the more violently he hated me. I gave up all hope that he would ever change and grow to like me because the disappointments were too frequent to be bearable. It was better to have no hope at all than to be let down every single time.

Chapter Five

Alex

In some ways at the beginning I liked the idea of being special to Dad, of being the only one in the family he was nice to. When he encouraged me to misbehave at school or not bother to go in at all, he made it sound much more interesting and exciting than it ever turned out to be, particularly as he was always generous with his bribes, giving me sweets or money if I did what he wanted. The more he could encourage me to misbehave, the more he knew he would annoy Mum and undermine all her efforts to keep me working hard and in the top classes for every subject. Annoying Mum and Isobel was the primary aim of almost everything he ever did in the house. I never stopped to question why; that's just the way it was.

At the same time I also discovered that however much he might pretend to me that we were allies when we were alone, he couldn't be trusted not to betray me as soon as he had an opportunity. He would encourage me to do something bad when it was just the two of us together, but as soon as Mum came home he would sneak on me and tell her what I had been doing, without confessing that he had suggested it in the first place. He would gloat over how badly behaved her precious little son really was, and how he had managed to sabotage all her good work in bringing me up. I never protested in my defence because I didn't want to provoke his anger and make him hate me as much as he hated the others, and because I was never one for protesting about things generally. I was always pretty philosophical about life, even as a small boy.

I soon learned that everything Dad did was part of some spiteful mind game he had dreamed up in the long hours he spent on his own in his room. If ever he gave us a present there was always a reason, a hidden agenda behind it. He heard Isobel asking Mum for money for something one day and so he put forty pounds in her room for her to find. Not knowing what to say, Isobel spent it and then a week or two later he demanded it back. Since Isobel only received a pound or two a week as pocket money, that took a long time and was something else for him to hold against her, another way to keep control and prove to her what a bad daughter she was.

He gave us both CD players one time, but only so he could smash Isobel's up in front of her and enjoy the look

43

of disappointment on her face. He must have planned it from the start because the one he bought me was far more expensive than the one he intended to destroy. When he first gave it to her Isobel sensed there was something wrong and was hesitant to even touch it for fear that it would prove to be a trap. When he smashed it he didn't even bother to say why, but I knew he wouldn't touch mine. I think he was always hoping to turn Isobel and me against one another, but that never worked.

Whatever he did to us Isobel and I were always a team. We had been together since the day I was born and we understood each other perfectly. No one could ever come between us, no matter how devious and cunning they might be. Although we had our own separate friends, we were often together socially as well. Isobel was always a bit of a tomboy and quite happy to hang out with groups of boys, playing football or climbing trees. She wasn't interested in whatever it was most of the girls wanted to do, which usually meant staying indoors as far as she could see. As we got older Mum didn't mind letting us go out to play with other kids in the area so long as we had finished our homework and so long as we were together. Not that we had very much spare time to just play around, because she filled virtually every waking hour with activities. If we did have a few spare hours, however, playing outside was always preferable to being indoors and worrying about disturbing Dad if we made any sort of noise at all. We didn't often take friends back home either because we could never be sure if he would be there or not, and if he did emerge from his room and find other people in the house he would always make a scene to ensure they felt as uncomfortable as possible.

'Our Dad might be there,' we would warn them on the odd occasions when we did bring friends back to the house. 'If he's there, just ignore him. Don't say anything to him if he talks to you.'

It was like warning children not to pet an unreliable dog in case it suddenly turned nasty and bit them. It was obvious that our friends couldn't understand why we were issuing warnings like this and I dare say they went back home to their own parents with some colourful descriptions of what the atmosphere was like inside our house, with the invisible bogeyman of a father hiding away upstairs, a bit like the wicked giant in 'Jack and the Beanstalk'. Most of the people we met during our after-school activities didn't even realise we had a dad since they only ever saw us out and about with Mum. He would never come to see us playing in a concert or competing in a sports match. Just like Mum, neither Isobel nor I would ever talk about him to other people if we didn't have to.

If Dad did make an appearance when there were other people in the house he would usually appear quite alarming. He seemed to take pride in making himself look as much of a thug as he could, and he wouldn't say much, just looming there, silent and threatening. On the rare occasions when he came to one or other of our activities he would be deliberately aggressive and abusive to everyone else there, as if he wanted to embarrass us and Mum, to teach us a lesson for taking an interest in something that was nothing to do with him and to show us who was in control. He liked to demonstrate his contempt for anything any of us did, to make it look as though Mum was wasting her time rushing around doing things that he thought were pointless and laughable. If you can't see the point in anything then there really isn't any reason to come out of your bedroom, especially if someone else is willing to pay the bills and provide you with food.

Mum would cook big meals when she had the time. Most Sundays she would do a family roast, although Dad still wouldn't want to come down to eat with us. He didn't even eat with us on Christmas Day. It didn't bother Isobel or me because we couldn't remember anything different, and it was always nicer when he wasn't around to create a bad atmosphere anyway, but it must have been hard for Mum. She must have wished she had a normal husband who was part of the family. She pretended not to notice that anything was wrong, keeping herself and us so busy that we didn't have too much time for introspection, but it must have been wearing her away inside.

On weeknights Isobel and I made sure we'd done our homework by the time Mum got home, and sorted out something to eat. We got through a lot of pasta in those years because there was never any time to cook anything more elaborate. There was certainly no space in our lives for just sitting down and relaxing over a meal. Mum drank endless cups of strong coffee throughout the day – sometimes as many as twenty a day – just to keep herself awake. Dad never ate the meals we prepared, of course. From what I could make out, he seemed to survive on takeaway kebabs or chips.

Mum was a great believer in the importance of exams and achieving things academically. During the daily car rides back and forth between after-school activities she would constantly bombard us with questions about school, getting us to go through every lesson and tell her what we had been learning and then she would fire questions at us, testing us on our times tables or our French vocabulary. She was always enthusiastic in the early days before tiredness started to overpower her, wanting to exercise our brains to the full at every opportunity. During half terms and holidays she would give us her own work projects and tests on top of anything our teachers might have set us. We never complained because we were so used to it and we knew she would always let us go out to play as soon as we had finished our work. We enjoyed most of the tasks anyway.

We certainly never had any time to chill out in front of the television as many of our friends did after school. None of this bothered us because we had never had a chance to get into the habit of watching television and whenever we did tune in the programmes seemed boring compared to the pace and variety of our own lives. The only time we might watch anything would be on a Sunday morning, but even then Mum wasn't that keen if there was something else she thought we should be doing, and we weren't interested enough to go against her wishes. About once a week we would catch an episode of *The Simpsons*, which was the only show we really liked.

From as early as I can remember, Mum would enrol us for every after-school activity imaginable. It didn't matter how much it cost (and they were virtually all private lessons), or how many hours of her evening she had to give up to ferry us from one place to another. She was determined that we should be given every possible opportunity to try everything, even if we decided not to follow it up later, and that we would never be unable to do something just because we couldn't afford it. Almost the moment she arrived home each afternoon, having driven for at least an hour back from work, she would be piling us into the little Metro she'd had for years and driving me to one place and Isobel to another.

The activities she enrolled us for covered virtually every skill she could think of. It wasn't just the musical instruments – piano, violin – and singing in the choir; there were also the physical activities like swimming and gymnastics, ballet and karate. If we tried something and didn't like it she would be happy to let us stop, but would immediately suggest something else instead. We must have belonged to every single club within a ten-mile radius of the house. At one stage I tried learning the trumpet but the teacher said I would do better changing to the French horn, which was a big instrument for a small boy to have to lug around with him all day. I joined the scouts but somehow Isobel escaped brownies and girl guides; I think maybe she didn't have enough hours left in her day to fit them in, although she did do woodcraft.

Isobel's favourite activity was running and she was brilliant at long distance and cross-country. She actually enjoyed going through the thickest mud and deepest puddles. She was so good she went all the way up to compete at county level. She was always a real tomboy, preferring football to ballet. Mum was willing to indulge her in anything that she showed an interest in, even though she was the only girl on the football team, until things got too rough and Isobel broke her finger at one match. After that, Mum decided enough was enough.

When we got a little older and started to have minds of our own, one or other of us might announce that we

49

wanted to give up one of our activities. Sometimes Mum would react badly to this. Maybe she didn't like the idea that we were growing up and not totally within her control any more. When Isobel said one evening that she wanted to give up swimming in order to have more time for her running Mum went completely ballistic.

'All the money I've spent on swimming lessons,' she shouted, 'and you want to give it up just like that?'

She seemed to hate the idea of us limiting our options in any way, even though there obviously weren't enough hours in the week for us to do everything properly. I think Isobel's swimming costume got hurled out of the window during that row, which seemed a bit out of proportion. It may just have been Mum's exhaustion and pent-up frustrations about other things that made her explode like that rather than the actual announcement itself. Isobel was determined not to change her mind, although she felt very guilty about letting Mum down and upsetting her.

When I announced I had quit the church choir she went even more over the top. I was around eleven years old and going through a bit of a rebellious phase at the time. I had actually sworn at the choirmaster during the practice that evening, which had resulted in me being ordered out of the room. I stormed off and disappeared for a few hours. The choirmaster phoned home and so

Mum knew exactly what had happened and started ranting on to Isobel about me.

'I'm going to call social services,' she raved. 'I've got to get something done about that boy!'

By the time I finally walked in through the front door she had lathered herself up into a real state of fury, but I stuck to my guns about leaving the choir and refused to go back. I think I might have provoked the whole confrontation deliberately in order to give myself an excuse to leave, so Mum was right to be angry with me, but I was still shocked by the sheer force of her disappointment.

Part of Mum's motivation could have been to get us all out of the house and out of Dad's way as much as possible, which was fine by us. There were certain times of the day, usually in the later part of the afternoon, when he might wake up and emerge unexpectedly from his room, coming down to the kitchen to make himself some food. At those times he didn't want us anywhere around. He believed it was 'his time' and 'his space' and we would have to make ourselves scarce. The mere sight of Isobel or Mum would remind him how much he hated them and didn't want them around.

It was best for all of us if we weren't in the house at that time if we didn't want to risk inciting his anger. If we had a day off sick from school we had to be very careful not to be in the kitchen during periods that he considered to be 'his'. He spent as much of his life behind the bedroom door as possible. Isobel and I never ventured through it – we had barely even glimpsed through the crack when it was opened for him to go in or out – so we had no idea exactly what he did in there to entertain himself all day. We just dreaded the times when he was forced to come out into the real world in order to eat or go to the bathroom.

There were so many things for us to do outside the house that it wasn't a problem most days. As we got better at our various sports and activities Isobel and I were entered into competitions that were further away from home, and before I left the choir we would sometimes go on trips at weekends to sing at weddings in other churches or even cathedrals. Then we got paper rounds, which got us out of the house for a few hours on a Sunday morning and gave us some spending money of our own. Isobel got the round first, being older, and used it as another opportunity to go running, hauling a trolley behind her as she pounded the streets. When her weekend running commitments got too much, she handed the paper round on to me. The people who ran the newsagents were happy with that because it meant they could go on delivering the papers to the same address each week and they knew it was likely I would be reliable because Isobel had never let them down. The Sunday round was the best one to have because we didn't have to get up as early as the weekday people, who had to finish their deliveries before going to school, but we still got paid the same rate. Part of the job was to insert advertising leaflets before delivering them. I managed to convince Mum that it was harder for me to do that because I was left-handed so she used to help me, much to Isobel's annoyance.

Although doing so much meant our days often ended up being a bit of a rush, both Isobel and I were always happy to do whatever Mum suggested. It was the only way of life either of us could remember and large parts of our social lives revolved around the activities because that was where we made many of our friendships.

Compared to most boys my acts of rebellion were pretty minor, like talking in class or swearing at the choirmaster. I did bunk off school for a day now and again, but very seldom. To Mum, however, with her strict regime of education and self-improvement, this was a cardinal sin. She couldn't bear the thought that I was wasting even the smallest opportunity to get a good education. On one of the few occasions I did wander off, she came home early one day to get her car serviced and caught me and my friends outside the school. She marched us all firmly back in through the gates, even though it was nearly the end of the school day by then, which was not good for my street credibility. She almost always came home at the same time, so I couldn't believe my bad luck when I was caught on that occasion.

The school occasionally sent her letters about my general behaviour. She left before the post arrived in the mornings, so Isobel and I would try to intercept as many as we could before they reached her. Mum knew that I wasn't concentrating fully on my work, even though I was still in the top set for just about every subject, and she became more and more exasperated with me the further I dug my heels in and rebelled against authority. At one stage she threatened to move me to her school, knowing how embarrassing it would be to have a mother who was on the staff, and knowing that I wouldn't want to leave my friends. I knew it was an empty threat because she would never have done anything that might have endangered my education, so then she began threatening to send me to boarding school if I didn't behave better. Even though I knew the cost of it would have been completely beyond her means, I never wanted to call her bluff on that one. She could be very determined when she set her mind on something. As well as not wanting to leave my established group of friends, I wouldn't have wanted to be separated from Isobel.

'I'll go to boarding school,' Isobel piped up in the middle of the argument about me leaving the choir, which deflected Mum's wrath away from me for a while. Because of that interruption Isobel got kicked out of the house that night instead of me, even though she didn't have any shoes on at the time.

Mum must have been bottling up so much anger and resentment that when some little thing like the choir incident happened she would completely lose her cool. She even kicked the dog out with Isobel, as if that would teach us all some sort of lesson. Alfie must have thought it was a bit of an adventure to be allowed out for an extra walk without his lead. At moments like that I think the whole world must suddenly have seemed to be against her and she imagined for a moment that she wanted to be rid of the lot of us. Her moods never lasted long, though – not like Dad's endless, snarling misery.

Whenever Dad got to hear about me doing anything remotely naughty or rebellious he would be delighted and would encourage me, deliberately going against everything Mum was saying. He seemed determined to make me more like him and less like her and Isobel. I don't know that his encouragement made much difference to me. I think I would have been behaving the same anyway, but it did give me a bit more courage to be cheeky at school, knowing that it won his approval. Every small boy wants to please his dad, even when he's as weird as mine was. Once or twice I even went back to the house during the day with my friends when we should have been in school, and Dad seemed to approve, which impressed them. But as soon as Mum came home he told her all about it, wanting to rub her nose in how much she had lost control of me, I guess, and how her children weren't always the hard-working little angels she would have liked them to be.

The strain on her during those years must have been enormous, and we didn't know the half of it at that stage. I feel guilty when I look back now, but I was just being a normal, spirited teenage boy. In retrospect I guess her life was hard enough without that additional pressure.

Chapter Six

Isobel

The row started because Alex had got himself thrown out of choir practice and then announced he wanted to leave the choir altogether, but for some reason I was the one who ended up being thrown out of the house by Mum. Things just went completely mad for a few minutes.

As I stood outside on the drive in my socks, holding onto Alfie by the scruff of his neck, I wasn't sure what to do next. Mum was in such a hysterical state that there didn't seem to be any point in trying to get back in the house until she had calmed down. The only person I could think of to turn to for help was my godmother, Helen, who had moved away from our street by then but was still living in the area. I don't think we had mobile phones at that stage – or at least if we did I didn't have one on me, not having expected to be leaving the house quite so abruptly – so I had to knock on one of the neighbours' doors and ask if I could use their house phone.

I don't think they were surprised by the request because everyone in the nearby houses knew about Dad and assumed that our whole family was a bit dysfunctional. I rang Helen, who very kindly came and took Alfie and me back to her house before going to talk to Mum and attempting to calm her down and make her see sense. Helen was a good friend to Mum and one of the few people she allowed to get close to her. I expect Mum was already regretting her outburst by the time Helen got there. These sorts of temper storms always passed quite quickly and we would then return to our normal family routines as if nothing had happened, the hectic pace of our lives helping us to forget any lingering bad feelings. Dad wouldn't usually come out of his room when Mum was kicking off. He had his own demons to fight in private. He had no interest in anything to do with any of us unless it affected him directly, and if Mum sounded upset that probably pleased him since he spent most of his time trying to achieve exactly that result.

I can't remember a time when I didn't know how much Dad hated me. It started because I looked so much like Mum, or at least that was what he kept telling me, but it grew worse as I got older and started speaking out against him more often. He needed to be able to dominate everyone in his life completely, and Mum was mostly willing to let him get away with it in order to protect us and try to maintain a fragile peace in the

no one listened

house. As I entered my teens, however, I became less willing to put up with everything he did in silence. If he was attacking Mum I would often take her side, speaking up for her while she remained silent, and that made him loathe me all the more deeply. Arguments were usually based on him saying how dirty the house was, or that the vacuum cleaner hadn't been put back in the right way, which was infuriating to me. The house was perfectly clean because Mum spent her weekends cleaning it, but nothing she did was ever right it seemed. It drove me crazy that Dad should have the nerve to complain when he sat around at home all day never lifting a finger.

Sometimes his attacks would escalate beyond mere shouting and he became physically violent. He would slap her and throw things at her while she tried frantically to pacify him by agreeing with everything he said, accepting all the criticism without trying to defend herself. Partly out of anger and partly out of fear, I would be screaming at him to leave her alone and threatening to call the police. He found the thought that I would dare to stand up to him almost unbearable and Mum would become desperate that I was winding him up even more by challenging him, but I couldn't just stand by and watch him hitting her without saying anything. Perhaps her approach was more intelligent than mine. Maybe she already sensed just what he might be capable of if he was pushed too far, but to me at the time, with all the recklessness and ignorance of youth, it looked as though she was giving in to him, being a complete doormat, and my pride wouldn't let me do the same.

On several occasions as I went to pick up the phone to call the police, Dad pushed me out of the way, threw an ornament at me, or lunged past me and ripped it out of the wall. He didn't always manage to get there in time, however, and when I was eleven or twelve years old I managed to call them out on two separate occasions. Both times I truly believed that Mum was in real danger and needed grown-up help. Once I heard noises from my bedroom and came downstairs to find him punching her and throwing her around the room. I intervened and he swung a punch at me as well. I managed to get a call through to the police but in the few minutes it took them to turn up he had wrecked the house in his frustration and fury.

Even when the police were standing there in the room and she had a chance to tell them what he was like, Mum would never make a formal complaint or agree to press charges, so there was nothing they could do apart from warn him to calm down. On one occasion when he was particularly wild they took him down to the cells for a few hours to give him time to settle down, only allowing him home once they felt he was calm again. I remember we were all terrified that they would release him in the middle of the night. Alex and I were literally shaking with fear so all three of us slept in my bed till morning. Locking him up served the purpose at the time but did nothing to help our overall situation. His was a vendetta of hate that would outlast any short-term measures the police might be able to impose.

When he got home after his night in the cells we were out at our swimming practice with Mum and by the time we arrived back he had changed all the locks on the house so our keys didn't work. Mum had to beg him through the letterbox to let us in, trying to avoid provoking a scene on the doorstep that the neighbours would hear. I suppose ultimately he had to let Mum back into the house because she was his only source of income, but he had made his point, showing that he could take control, lock us out and disrupt our lives whenever he chose if we displeased him or challenged him.

On one of the occasions when I called the police Dad ran upstairs and started stabbing himself in the arm with a fork so that when they arrived he could tell them that Mum had attacked him first, and show them the wounds to prove it. When they got there the police left Alex and me sitting on the stairs, just watching and listening and taking it all in. They didn't ask us for our version of what had gone on, but just ignored us as if we were part of the furniture. Maybe they get called to so many domestic disturbances every day that they have a set method of dealing with them, but they never made us feel that they would be able to offer us or Mum any real protection from Dad should we need it. Later, when we were in court for Dad's trial, a policeman read out his notes of the incident that night, talking about 'two young and clearly very disturbed children' being on the scene. If we were so clearly disturbed, why didn't anyone do anything to help us, or even talk to us? Why did no one come back the next day after one of these fights to check we were okay? I suppose by not pressing charges Mum forced them to assume that she had the whole situation under control.

Most of the arguments happened late at night, when Dad would emerge from his room and expect to have the house to himself, or perhaps he would decide to go and waken Mum to raise some grudge he had been mulling over all day. Looking back, Dad was getting through a lot of whisky and I suspect the worst arguments probably happened when he was drunk. Alex was usually fast asleep by the time they started to shout and often didn't wake up, allowing Dad to believe that he could still control him and keep him on his side, even if I was becoming openly rebellious to his tyranny.

If Mum was still up and about when Dad got downstairs it was almost inevitable that he would start picking a fight with her. Most of the time our routines meant that we were able to avoid him, but if something went differently it would make him feel threatened and he would immediately become aggressive. Sometimes, if he had fuelled himself up enough on whisky, he would keep the arguments going all night, forcing Mum to stay awake just so that he could shout at her, and me as well when I came downstairs to investigate. It didn't bother him how long the fights went on for because he could just sleep through the next day, but we were exhausted and needed our sleep. He knew perfectly well how tired Mum got and exploited it sadistically. I think sometimes he picked fights simply to alleviate the boredom of his existence.

As he got older Alex started to be woken by the shouting as well and we would all end up only getting a couple of hours sleep, but however tired we were in the morning Mum would never consider for a second that we should be allowed a day off school. It was almost like a religious belief to her. She would never take a day off work, however ill or exhausted she felt, and she expected the same level of dedication, determination and discipline from us. We didn't even bother to ask because we knew what her answer would be. I think my attendance rate was pretty close to a hundred per cent and Alex only managed to bunk off once or twice before Mum found out and put a stop to it. To be honest we were always pretty keen to get out of the house after a night of rowing anyway. We certainly didn't want to be trapped there on our own with Dad if we could help it. Once we were with our friends at school, or concentrating in lessons, we could forget for a few hours the unpleasant things we had been forced to listen to in the small hours.

Even when Mum was left with bruises or marks on her face and arms from his beatings she would still go to work, telling colleagues that she had walked into a door or some such excuse, and we later discovered from Jillian that no one ever doubted her for a moment. No one at her school had the slightest idea that she was in an abusive relationship. Jillian and a couple of others knew she was married to a man who was odd, but most of them thought she was a single mother and never enquired any further. I suppose she just wasn't the sort of person you would ever expect to be in that position, because she always seemed so vibrant and in control of every detail of her life.

The only people who I believe knew there was violence going on, and suspected that it was much worse than Mum was saying, were my godmother Helen and the lady vicar at our local church. They were the only two people Mum talked to about it and we discovered that both of them tried to persuade her to leave Dad before things got any worse. Near neighbours later testified that they could hear arguments going on all the time, but none of them wanted to interfere because Dad was such a frightening figure and because Mum seemed to be so capable and seemed to want to keep everything private. When our next-door neighbour on the other side from the old lady was asked why she had never called the police during any of the rows she said that it was because she and her husband were having their own marital problems at the time. Mum never wanted to make a fuss about anything. Perhaps if she had been a little less strong-willed and a little more willing to accept help she would still be alive today.

Mum was a keen churchgoer and would attend every Sunday. When Alex and I were both in the choir we spent even more time there, which could be boring at times although we had a lot of friends there. The biggest bonus to being in the choir was that occasionally we would get paid a few pounds for singing at a wedding. Mum was very proud of us because we got to visit all sorts of cathedrals around the country and once even went on a choir holiday to Wales. We both sang solos so I suppose we must have had pretty good voices.

I think Mum had strong Christian beliefs, although she didn't talk about them much, and maybe that was another reason why she believed she had to soldier on with the marriage 'for better or worse'. In her eyes she had made a commitment to my Dad and she was never one to weaken once she had done that. When I started to learn more about religion at school I would sometimes challenge her on her beliefs, like a typical teenager, but she never rose to the bait. Maybe she just went to church because she always had done and she liked the discipline and routine of it.

Although she and Dad hadn't done anything about having us baptised when we were born, she wanted us to be able to get confirmed at the same time as our friends at the church, so we wouldn't feel like odd ones out. She arranged for us to be baptised when I was about twelve and Alex was about ten and that was when she asked Helen and Steve to be our godparents. Dad wasn't remotely interested in any of it and didn't even turn up for the service.

Mum was the strongest person imaginable considering all she had to put up with, but eventually even she found the pressure too much. One night, after one of Dad's all-night attacks on her, she decided to commit suicide. I was fourteen at the time. We had no idea how bad things had got inside her head and we would certainly never have thought she would consider the option of suicide for even a second. I will never know exactly what was going through her mind on the night she made the decision, although I found out a lot more later that she hadn't told us at the time, but it was a decision she took with all her usual pragmatism and lack of emotion.

It must have been a really hard decision for her on a number of levels. Firstly there were her religious beliefs to overcome, and I also don't believe she would ever have taken the idea of leaving Alex and me with Dad lightly. She must have wrestled with her conscience for a long time before deciding to do it.

Perhaps her mind was clouded by the exhaustion she was obviously suffering from at the time. It must have been a relatively quiet fight she had with Dad that night because Alex and I both slept right through it. She must have stayed awake even after he had finally run out of steam and gone back to his room. Everything must have seemed so impossibly bleak as she sat on her own downstairs in the small hours of the morning, in the dark silent house. I found out later, long after the event, that she had serious health problems, although she hadn't told us at that stage, and she maybe thought that by ending things quickly she was sparing us from having to see her suffer and die slowly.

She had some tablets, but I don't know if that was a co-incidence or if she had been saving them up deliberately. We were told later she took eighty-six pills, a mixture of paracetamol and whatever else she could find in the house, which seems an awful lot unless you have been deliberately hording them. Even in her moment of deepest despair she wanted to cause us the minimum amount of trauma possible. She didn't want us to be the ones to find her, so as soon as she had swallowed the tablets she quietly let herself out of the house and went for a walk across the Downs.

It was a bitterly cold morning so maybe it was the fresh air, perhaps combined with the beauty of the rising sun, that shook her out of her black mood and made her realise that she had made a mistake and that she couldn't abandon Alex and me. Whatever it was that changed her mind she turned round and hurried home, determined to get help before the tablets started to take effect. When she got back she rang Helen and asked her to come to the house to help. The sounds of their raised voices woke me. I could sense an air of panic and I came downstairs to find out what was going on. Helen was trying to ring an ambulance on the house phone. She told me the truth about what had happened but we decided just to tell Alex that Mum was feeling ill without going into any details.

'Your phone's not working,' Helen said, unable to keep the tone of panic from her voice.

'Dad ripped it out of the wall the other day,' I told her.

'I'll have to drive your mother to the hospital,' she said.

There was no option but to keep to our usual routine because Mum wouldn't hear of anything else. As usual Alex didn't ask too many questions when he came down, just watching what was going on around him with patient, solemn eyes, so I didn't have to lie to him as we got ready and walked to school as if it was any other day. He was good like that, always willing to wait until things came clear, never in a rush. When we got home that

afternoon Mum still wasn't back from hospital. We kept
as quiet as we could while we made ourselves something
to eat and did our homework, so as not to aggravate Dad
and bring him storming out of his room. We knew all
the routines to follow until Mum returned. She came
home from the hospital later the same day but she was
still throwing up constantly and I'm afraid I wasn't very
sympathetic.

'How could you do that to yourself?' I yelled, furious
with her at the thought of how she had been willing to
leave us at Dad's mercy without even preparing us for
the shock, and hurt as well. I was so angry I couldn't
bring myself to offer to help her even though she was
obviously feeling really ill.

'You must be nice to her,' Helen said when she came
round, bustling about, trying to keep the mood cheerful.

'Why?' I wanted to know. 'She's brought this whole
thing on herself.'

Helen didn't answer. Mum couldn't give me any
explanation as to what she had been thinking, still not
willing to talk about all the worries that must have been
weighing her down by then. Maybe she didn't want to
burden me, or perhaps she knew she wouldn't be able to
put them into words without making herself cry, which
she wouldn't have wanted to do.

'I knew you would both be okay. You're old enough
to look after Alex now,' was all the justification she was

willing to give when she was finally feeling strong enough to reply to my open hostility.

With the benefit of hindsight I think she was also worried that she would become an invalid and didn't want to get to the stage where we had to look after her, as well as having to cope with Dad's increasing aggression, but Alex and I didn't know anything about the gravity of her illnesses at that stage. She must have believed that if she died social services would become involved and they would make sure we were okay. Again with the benefit of hindsight, I wouldn't be able to share that confidence.

'I'm going to leave when you're sixteen anyway,' she said in another surprise announcement, but then refused to explain what she meant. I didn't challenge her because it sounded as though she really meant it and I wasn't sure I wanted to know any more. At the time I assumed she meant she would make another suicide attempt when I was sixteen, but perhaps she was thinking she would just walk out and leave us. That seems even harder to imagine somehow. The subject was never mentioned again, like so many things in our family. It is hard to grasp just how deeply depressed she must have been, but to try to take her own life was so far out of character that things must have been very bad indeed.

I didn't know what to think; I just knew I didn't want her to go. Despite my bravado with Dad when she was around, I was deeply frightened of him and didn't like being in the house on my own with him – which was one of the reasons why my school attendance record was as good as it was. The only time I can remember being forced to stay at home during a school day was when the arch of my foot collapsed and I literally couldn't stand on it at all, so I couldn't even hobble into work with Mum. I had to rest for a couple of days, unable to leave the house, and I was terrified that Dad would get up and come down to the kitchen and I would get in his way and impinge on his territory. Being alone in the house with him was the worst feeling imaginable, because I never knew what would happen if I accidentally annoyed him. While he was still safely asleep I set myself up in the living room with drinks and everything I would need in order to last without having to come out until Mum or Alex got home.

I tried to avoid ever being on my own with him, because I knew how much he hated me and how spiteful he could be. Two or three times, when Mum was away for any reason, he decided to cook a meal for us. This might sound as though he was making an effort to be a good father but he had a theory that oil was good for us and he would smother the food so thickly in it that it would be inedible. Apparently he had been diagnosed with high cholesterol and believed olive oil would help him to avoid suffering another stroke. He would insist that we swallowed every mouthful of whatever he had prepared and became very aggressive when he saw that we were struggling to finish what was on our plates. We often worried that he might have poisoned the food and that fear made every mouthful an ordeal. Once the meal was over and he had disappeared back into his room we would sit and wait to see if anything happened to us. It was such a rare thing for him to cook for us we felt sure he must have an ulterior motive.

Sometimes his displays of spite would be completely childish. On cold winter days, for instance, when he decided to open all the doors and windows, I'm sure that he deliberately wanted to make us suffer, just to show that he could. Alex and I would have to huddle up close to the airing cupboard to try to keep warm while we did our homework.

I thought I was coping pretty well with all the trouble at home but around about the age of twelve, I began to become obsessed with washing my hands all the time and counting inside my head. I liked the number four the best – even numbers were always my favourites, and four most of all. I decided that I would wash my hands forty-four times a day, since four wasn't enough, and that's what I began to do. Before long, it was driving Mum crazy. We were always running out of soap and my hands were red and painful from all the scrubbing, but I only felt comfortable when I reached the forty-fourth handwash of the day. It was only years later that psychologists diagnosed my handwashing as a symptom of obsessive-compulsive disorder and said it probably resulted from the stress of all the arguments and violence I witnessed at home.

The stress of living with Dad must also have been wearing Mum down as surely as the physical exhaustion of always being on the go and never having a comfortable night's sleep or a relaxed meal. There is a limit to how much tiredness any body can bear before it starts to wear out. But the problems with Dad and the stress of our day-to-day routines were only the tip of the iceberg. Mum had far more than that to contend with, as we were soon to find out.

Shortly after Mum's suicide attempt I did something really stupid and tried to steal some clothes from a shop. I really needed some new stuff and I didn't have the heart to mention it to Mum, knowing how bad she would feel at not being able to give me everything I needed, however hard she tried. She had enough on her plate so I thought I would solve the problem myself. A lot of the other kids at school talked about pinching things from shops as if it was the most normal thing in the world and for a mad moment I thought perhaps I was the odd one out for always working so hard to earn every penny I needed, and maybe I should just take what I needed like everyone else.

I must have been a terrible shoplifter, made clumsy by my guilty conscience and my wildly thumping heart, because I was immediately caught and marched off to the police station. They called home to speak to Mum and Dad took a message, but didn't do anything about it. I can imagine how pleased he must have been to discover that I had gone off the rails and let Mum down so spectacularly. He must have got immense pleasure from telling her the news the moment she walked in the door from work.

Mum deliberately didn't turn up to collect me from the police station for six hours, leaving me to sit all alone in a bare cell listening to the threatening shouts of a load of indignant drunks. She knew exactly what she was doing because I was absolutely petrified as I sat shivering in my cell. There was no way I was ever going to repeat this mistake. As a girl who never liked to be anything but first at everything I did, I had suddenly sunk to being a failed petty criminal, the lowest of the low in the eyes of the security guard, the manager at the shop and the policemen who took me in – at least that was how it seemed to me.

When Mum did finally turn up in the cell I have never been so pleased to see anyone in my life, even though she was furious and started giving me a really hard time the moment she came through the door. In fact she was yelling so loudly the police, who were used

74

to dealing with stroppy fourteen-year-olds, thought it was me shouting at her rather than the other way round and gave me another telling off for being rude to my mother.

Once we had got home and she had calmed down a bit, Mum stopped shouting at me and started blaming herself instead, saying she wasn't a good enough mother to us – which made me feel even worse about what I'd done. Because so many people in my year at school went shoplifting regularly it hadn't actually seemed such a big deal when I set out but it had degenerated into a nightmare, leaving me feeling as though I had failed and let her down as well as myself. The school got to hear about it and we had to go in together to see the headmaster. Because I was a straight 'A' student and had never previously got into any trouble he was a bit surprised and disappointed to hear what I'd been up to.

'Is everything all right at home?' he asked kindly, obviously assuming there must be another reason for my strange behaviour beyond any sudden need I might have felt to refresh my wardrobe. I didn't have time to say a word before Mum jumped in quickly with an adamant denial, so I could hardly contradict her and make it sound as though she was a liar or a bad mother. It could have been a good opportunity for her to come clean and explain that we had some real problems in the family because of Dad's behaviour, and that she had recently

75

been driven to attempting suicide – but even then she couldn't do it, couldn't talk about something so personal. Instead she took all the blame for my fall from grace, telling him it was her fault for being an inadequate mother and not being around enough for us. I doubt that the headmaster was convinced by that because everyone knew how much she did for us, but he let it pass. No further action was taken but I still had to pay a price for my stupidity. I got a reprimand from the police, which still pops up every time I ever go for a job interview even though it should have been wiped from my record as soon as I turned eighteen. I keep being told that it shouldn't happen, but it does. The one time I tried to break the law and it seems to be haunting me forever.

We only found out what was going on inside Mum's head when she had no option but to tell us. The suicide attempt had been a huge shock, and not long afterwards she was forced to tell us that she had cancer. Before that she had decided not to mention it to anyone apart from the doctors who were treating her. It wasn't until the day she was being admitted to hospital for an operation to remove a lump from her breast that she finally told Alex and me what was going on.

'I'm going into hospital today for an operation,' she said over breakfast. 'It's breast cancer. You'll be staying with Helen and Steve for a couple of days. If you have any questions, look in these leaflets.'

I accepted the pile of leaflets she handed over, too shocked to say much. This was the first we had heard about her being ill at all. There must have been numerous doctors' appointments, scans and tests going on over the previous weeks and months, all of which she had managed to keep hidden from us. We had no idea how long she had known or how serious it might be, but it did give us another clue as to why she might have been so stressed and exhausted recently. Even now she only told us the barest facts, without any elaboration. She still wasn't telling us how she felt about her illness or what the prognosis might be. She didn't offer us any grains of comfort, or give us any opportunity to comfort her. Such considerations wouldn't have entered her head. She simply told us the facts and gave us some leaflets to read should we wish to find out more about breast cancer.

Mum was never very physically or emotionally demonstrative, so Alex and I had become the same way. I wish I had given her a big hug that morning when she told us about the cancer, but it wasn't the way we'd been brought up. I never used to go to her to talk about things that were worrying me. She wouldn't have known how to comfort me anyway; she always looked for practical solutions to any problems and would have counselled me 'not to make a fuss' or 'just get on with it'. I suppose working for so many years as a teacher meant she had seen it all and heard it all and knew that none of the problems of childhood were as serious as they seemed to the child in question, but still it would have been nice if we could have talked more about our feelings and worries from time to time.

With hindsight I wonder if bottling up so many emotions and not talking to anyone about her worries was one of the reasons she got ill. At least Alex and I had each other to talk to when we needed to let off steam, although we had both learned from her example early on and tended not to get emotional about many things.

She wrote to her bosses at school, explaining simply that she was going for an operation and telling them how long she would be off work. She had always scheduled any doctors' or dentists' appointments for late in the day so she would cause the minimum amount of disruption to the school timetable, and she behaved in exactly the same way about the operation. She gave them a detailed description of everything that was going on in each of her classes and of the contingency plans she had made to help the replacement teachers who would have to fill in for her, and she passed all her own textbooks on to them. She guaranteed she would be back in the classroom the first moment she was able. I wonder if perhaps she was frightened to stay off work for too long because then she would have had time to think about things. The fact that she had tried to kill herself suggests that there was a depression just waiting to engulf her if she sat still for long enough to allow it to take hold. As long as she was busy and following a hectic routine there was no chance to dwell on how unhappy she was and just how hopeless it all seemed.

As with everything in her life she stuck only to the facts and the practicalities of the situation and ignored any possible emotional consequences. She wanted no sympathy and no special treatment; she could have been talking about a routine but unavoidable visit to the dentist.

In a way her unemotional approach to news that could have been very traumatic made it easier for Alex and me to deal with. Although we were shocked and frightened by the news, we assumed that if she was being so calm about it then there couldn't be too much to worry about. Maybe the operation was no more than a formality, we told ourselves as we set off to school together as usual that morning. She had made it all sound so minor and casual that when we went into the hospital to visit her in the evening we were horrified to see all the tubes and machines around her bed. As we stood there taking it all in, it dawned on both of us at the same time that our mother had just been through a much more serious operation than we had imagined. But by then it was all over, so we could tell ourselves that she would be recovering soon, blocking out any worries or fears that might try to muscle in. So maybe her approach had some merit.

The nurses asked us to help them bath her the next day as she wasn't able to move her arms because of where she had been cut and stitched. It was good to be given a practical task and to be able to help make her more comfortable, but it was shocking to see the long, livid scar across her chest and into her armpit. Somehow, looking at that, I couldn't imagine she would be back to her old self as quickly as she was promising. The terrifying thought flashed across my mind that maybe this cancer was going to kill her, but I quickly shoved it away and refused to let myself think that way. The prospect was just too awful to contemplate.

Chapter Seven

Alex

We have no idea whether Mum's cancer would have come back or whether it would have eventually killed her because less than a year later Dad had murdered her. We know she went back for follow-up treatments after the operation, but she never talked about them, apart from giving us information about the times of her appointments so that we could make practical arrangements to continue our own lives as normal around her absences. We had no idea whether the doctors believed the treatments were working or not. I guess they probably didn't know at that stage either. As usual we didn't ask her any questions; we weren't sure how to phrase them anyway. I suppose I didn't want to know if it was bad news, preferring to think that as long as she wasn't saying anything to the contrary, we could assume she was fine. We were all sticking our heads in the sand like a family of ostriches.

Once she came out of hospital Mum just got on with life in exactly the same way she always had, so we did the same. When she arrived home after the operation she went back to sleeping downstairs on the couch, even though it was too short for her to be able to lie out flat and it must have been incredibly uncomfortable for her with the stitches. The pain caused her to moan in her sleep at night, which got on Dad's nerves and made him shout and curse. Even though he was complaining that she was making a noise and disturbing his peace and quiet, it didn't occur to him to offer her his bed or to do anything that would help her be more comfortable. Fear of upsetting him gave her another reason to keep as quiet as she could about whatever was troubling her. He hated her so deeply by that stage that he was happy to let her suffer as long as she didn't make a noise and disturb him.

'Please take one of our beds,' Isobel and I both begged. 'We'll be fine on the couch.'

But she wouldn't hear of it. The most important thing to her was our schoolwork, which meant we needed to sleep well in order to be wide-awake in the mornings for our lessons. In every way possible she sacrificed her own health, comfort and happiness for us, determined to give us every possible chance of succeeding in life. The only time she would ever agree to use one of our beds was if we were away sleeping at a friend's house.

But even Mum was forced to make a few concessions to the physical effects of the operation. She let us do the shopping for her for a few weeks because she wasn't strong enough to carry heavy bags, but that was the only interruption she would allow to our normal routine. During the week after the operation she was sitting on the couch marking the piles of school books that she had brought home with her, and the week after that she had gone back to teaching part-time to ensure her students missed as little of their curriculum as possible.

Looking back now I wonder if all the stress and worry she had to put up with was a contributing factor in causing the cancer. She lost a lot of weight and became stick thin and constantly tired-looking towards the end of her life. Where once she had taken care to look smart and tidy whenever she went out of the house, she eventually gave up bothering, pulling on whatever clothes came to hand and making no effort with her appearance. Just getting through each day seemed to take all the energy she could muster.

I can't remember her ever spending any money on herself apart from absolute essentials. Although she must have earned a decent salary as a head of department, the expense of paying for all our after-school activities left nothing for her to spend on clothes or luxuries like make-up or hairdressers. She also had to supply Dad with a never-ending stream of alcohol as well as paying the mortgage and food and petrol bills. Every day she seemed to bring him another bottle of whisky, which he would take back into his room to drink alone without a

word, escaping from the world into an alcoholic stupor.
I don't know if she hoped that giving him everything he
demanded would make him be nicer to her, or whether
she was just too frightened of him to say no. Maybe she
simply believed it was the best chance she had of having
a quiet life. Perhaps in the end it had just become a habit.

The lack of spare money was evident inside the house
too, where we never had any new furniture or decora-
tion. We couldn't afford to pay a decorator and we
certainly didn't have time to do any painting ourselves.
Mum kept the place as clean and neat as she could in the
time available to her, but she didn't waste any of her
precious financial resources on doing anything up. It was
as if she was pouring every last ounce of her energy into
her job and into our future, draining herself dry in the
process. As well as having to pay for her own travel costs
every day she also had to pay for Dad to have a car, plus
all the household bills. There wasn't any money left to
spend on treats or luxuries.

Even when it was obvious how much he hated her
and how badly their relationship had degenerated, Mum
kept trying to please Dad. She would still buy him
Christmas and birthday presents, even though he never
did the same for her and never uttered a word of thanks.
I guess the harder she tried to please him, the more he
grew to despise her. The more he came to depend on her,
the more he resented it.

He was continually attempting to find new ways to divide and rule the rest of us, trying to keep control of things. The telephone was one of his weapons. To spite Isobel and Mum he installed a line for me in my bedroom, and then fitted a lock to my door so that they couldn't get to it without him or me agreeing to let them in. It was a stupid, pointless exercise but none of us wanted to say anything and risk another row.

Alfie the dog hated Dad as much as the rest of us, always cowering away under the table whenever he heard his footsteps on the stairs. He even learned to fear Dad's name – Bert – running for cover if he heard it spoken out loud. If Mum, Isobel or I were in the room when Dad came in, however, Alfie would muster all his canine courage to stand in front of us, snarling a warning that he wouldn't allow us to be attacked. Dad hated him for that; he would have preferred to control him and turn him against us.

'I'm going to keep that dog in my room from now on,' he would threaten every time it happened, 'and train it to attack you.'

He never did that, of course, because he didn't actually want the bother of having Alfie in his room with him, so instead he took to teasing and bullying him in the same way he did us. He would bring in the ferrets he kept in the shed outside and encourage them to attack Alfie, trying to teach him who was boss in the house – as if Alfie didn't already know. Dad loved those ferrets and used to let them crawl up inside his sleeves or run around nipping at our heels. However much he intimidated Alfie, though, he couldn't completely break his spirit. Sometimes, if Alfie had particularly angered him he would chain him up outside and beat him with metal poles or anything else he could lay his hands on, leaving him whimpering in pain and covered in cuts.

It was heartbreaking for Isobel and me to watch, but for years we didn't have the courage to intervene, in case he turned his rage on us instead. As the years passed, though, we became braver and angrier. Once we were so incensed after finding Alfie had been beaten and chained again, we went into the garage and stole the offending poles. They felt so heavy and cruel it made us even more furious and for a few minutes we completely lost our cool. We ran upstairs with the poles and banged on Dad's bedroom door with them, shouting abuse at him. We couldn't be sure if he was in there or not, but he usually was. We would never have dared attempt to break down the door, which he kept locked. Luckily for us he didn't bother to respond to our provocation; maybe he enjoyed the idea that he had finally managed to get to us enough to provoke a reaction.

Mum would always try to quieten us down if we ever seemed about to challenge him; she was always looking for ways to prevent a full-scale confrontation. On that occasion our anger only lasted a few minutes before we came to our senses and backed away, hiding the poles near our beds in case he tried to attack us in the night. I think we just wanted to make a noise and express our unhappiness rather than actually break in to his room. I don't know what we would have done if we had burst through or if he had opened it and stormed out to face us down. We both knew his violence was getting worse.

I imagine Alfie received a lot of beatings and kickings while the rest of us were out of the house that we never knew about. I think sometimes the poor creature received the beatings that Dad would really have liked to be doling out to Mum and Isobel. If he ever barked during the day, which most dogs do from time to time, the noise would waken Dad up and he would charge downstairs to do something about it. He never stopped to find out what Alfie might be barking about; he just did his best to intimidate him into silence as quickly as possible. If we were in the house we would be trying to shut him up, our hearts racing with fear that Dad might burst in and attack either us or the dog, constantly straining our ears in case we heard him coming downstairs.

Just as it is with human beings, I think there are some dogs who are natural-born victims, and Alfie was definitely one of them. He was the meekest of animals, always being picked on by other dogs when we took him out for walks and often ending up having to be taken to the vet to get stitches in his wounds after fights. Our main concern when we got home from school was to get into the house quietly without disturbing Dad, but Alfie would be so excited to see us after spending all day alone he would start barking and we would have to shut him up as quickly as possible in case Dad was there.

There were days when we forgot our keys in the morning rush and when we got home in the afternoon we'd ring the doorbell to get in, but Dad completely ignored us. We'd be left outside until Mum got back to let us in, or until we managed to find a window we could wriggle through like cat burglars. On one of these occasions Isobel and I peered through the letterbox after ringing the bell and we could actually see Dad sitting in the kitchen, pretending he couldn't hear us. It was as if he was always trying to teach us a lesson for some reason or other.

Like us, Alfie seemed willing to put up with any amount of abuse from Dad in order to have a quiet life but eventually Dad overstepped the mark, and that was the day I finally stood up to him. I can't remember what Alfie had done to offend him in the first place, but whatever it was it resulted in Dad smashing him repeatedly around the head with a big heavy mixing bowl to 'teach him a lesson'. I was in the room at the time and watched in horror when Alfie finally reacted as Dad raised his hand to strike again by jumping up and biting it hard, taking out a massive chunk of flesh.

I knew that an act of defiance like that could push Dad to do something even more brutal and before I could stop myself I yelled at him, willing to risk bringing his wrath down on my own head rather than see him attacking the dog any more.

'Leave the fucking dog alone,' I shouted, and was surprised to see that he actually stopped in his tracks. It had never occurred to me before that I might be able to influence his behaviour in any way. I might have saved Alfie from getting a worse beating that day, but from that moment onwards Dad saw me as one of the enemy. I was no longer a potential ally to be used and manipulated in his war against the rest of them. If he couldn't control me and keep me on his side then he wanted to destroy me just as much as he wanted to destroy Mum and Isobel. I'd crossed the line.

Chapter Eight

Isobel

Mum was late getting up on the morning she died. I don't think she ever used an alarm in her life, always relying on her own body clock to wake her at the right moment, following years of the same routines. The more exhausted her body became, the harder it must have been for that instinct to work effectively, especially once she was ill with breast cancer. That Friday morning, the 11th of January 2002, it let her down completely. She succumbed to what must have been an overwhelming need to rest and was still deeply asleep on the couch when I came downstairs.

As always I was preoccupied with planning the rest of my day as I got ready to leave, working out what I needed to take and where I needed to be later. I remembered I had a piano lesson after school and I knew I would need to get myself there because Mum wouldn't be back from school in time to drive me. It wasn't a problem; I was fifteen years old now and I'd done it a thousand times before. If she knew she was coming back from work early for some reason she would offer to give me a lift, but she didn't say anything that morning as she rushed around, bleary-eyed, getting her books together and pulling on whatever clothes came to hand. I had no reason to think she would be there when I got home. Something unexpected must have happened to change her plans during the day; a moved hospital appointment, perhaps.

The routines of the school day passed exactly as normal, just the usual lessons and the usual socialising in between. There is nothing lodged in my memory that makes the school day stand out as any different from hundreds of others.

That afternoon, as we got ready to go home, my friend Katrina and I both discovered that our PE kit had gone missing. We kept them in our particular cubby holes on a shelf in the cloakroom and someone had been messing around and moved them. It wasn't that unusual an occurrence – just annoying, since I couldn't go home without it because I needed it for the weekend. We had to keep searching the changing rooms together until the missing items turned up. It was frustrating but stuff like that happens all the time at school.

We were talking to the PE teacher about things in general as we searched. I can't remember how the subject came up, but I remember saying, 'I think my Mum might die soon.'

I had mentioned my fears about Mum to teachers at school before and they had actually called her in to talk about it once, worried that I might have some deep-rooted anxieties. She had managed to brush aside my concerns, as she always did, and leave the teachers with the impression that there was nothing for anyone to worry about. She was good at that was Mum, always giving the outside world the impression that everything was fine in our family when it obviously wasn't. I don't know what made me make that strange little announcement that day, whether it was the suicide attempt, the cancer operation or her promise that she would be leaving as soon as I turned sixteen. Perhaps I was subconsciously preparing myself, trying to get used to the idea just in case any one of these things happened. I certainly wasn't expecting her to be killed and had no idea how prophetic my words would soon turn out to be.

The search for the PE kit made me a bit later than usual leaving the school premises, but I still had enough time to get home and do my homework before it would be time to go to piano, so I wasn't in any particular rush as I made my way across the main road towards our house.

The junction where I turned into our street was about eight houses away from home and the whole road was jammed full of police cars and ambulances and uniformed men rushing around as if they were on important and serious business. Because there were so many of them, at first I couldn't work out which house their attentions were centred on but my instincts told me it was probably something to do with us, because it always was. Whenever there was trouble in the street it was usually connected to Dad. 'What's he done now?' I wondered. Had he hung himself, as he was always threatening? I didn't have time to think about it logically and realise there were far too many people there for it to be just a suicide attempt. There were no fire engines so presumably he hadn't set fire to the house, which was his other regular threat.

As I walked on I noticed Mum's little red Nova, which she had recently traded the Metro for, was parked outside the house and I wondered what she was doing back home. She certainly hadn't said anything that morning about coming back early or I would have remembered. An uncomfortable knot of anxiety was growing inside me. Maybe all these people were here because of something to do with her. It couldn't just be a fight or a suicide bid; it had to be something major for this many people to turn out. I began to recognise the faces of neighbours amongst the policemen and medics milling around in the road. As I got closer to our front garden I realised that everyone was looking at me as if I was something to do with what was going on. Their expressions were strange – a mixture of curiosity, sympathy and shock. It started to feel like a very long walk before I would reach the point where I would be able to find out what had happened.

When I finally got to our front garden I saw Alex sitting on the wall with his usual patient, calm and slightly puzzled expression. He was surrounded by policemen, who seemed to be trying to stop him from going out to the road, even though he was showing no sign of wanting to go anywhere. One of the police cars drew away from the kerb as I got closer, my heart thumping in my ears. I could see a man in the back but I didn't realise till later that it was my father. By that time I must have been in some sort of state of shock as I tried to push my way through the crowd of men and uniforms to get to the house. The door was slightly ajar but I couldn't see inside.

'Where's the dog?' I demanded, unable to understand why Alfie wasn't barking at all these strangers invading his territory. 'Where's Mum? Why's her car here?'

Everyone was getting in my way, trying to block me from getting into the house to try to find out what was going on, but none of them were talking to me or answering any of my questions. They were just staring at me and then looking away in embarrassment when I caught their eyes. It was like a nightmare and I was becoming more and more annoyed and frustrated until eventually I lashed out at one of the policemen who was deliberately standing in my way. He caught my wrist just before my punch landed.

'If you do that we're going to have to put you in a police car,' he warned, 'and we really don't want to have to do that, do we?'

'Where's the dog?' I persisted, growing angry at being treated like this.

'He's in the kitchen,' the policeman said, although he obviously didn't know that.

'There's no door to the kitchen,' I snapped. 'He's not in the kitchen or he would have come out. Don't lie to me.'

I couldn't understand why these people were bothering to lie to me. Why wasn't anyone simply explaining to me what was going on in my own house? Where was Mum? Why wasn't she at work? Why was her car there? Why weren't they letting us past? Nothing was making sense. Why wasn't Alfie making his usual noise? Normally when he was in the dining room he was kept in with a little metal gate Dad had installed. I didn't realise the police had already taken that away because it had a massive dent in it, which they thought was relevant to whatever struggle had gone on. The police must have shut the door on Alfie to keep him contained. Maybe he was intimidated by so much going on around him, so many strange people and voices and noises. He was probably as frightened and confused as Alex and I were and that's why he wasn't barking. The more questions I asked, the more studiously they ignored me and I was

95

becoming increasingly agitated and worked up as I tried to get some straight answers. Why were they all lying to me? Why wouldn't anyone tell me what was happening?

The main thing I wanted was to be able to get into the house. The main thing the police wanted was to shut me up so they could get on with whatever their procedures were. Alex was still sitting on the wall, watching everything going on around him with wide eyes. It didn't look as though he had any more idea what was happening than I did. We caught eyes but didn't say anything to each other at that stage.

The police must have been praying that someone would find a family liaison officer soon so that they wouldn't have to listen to any more of my questions and could get both of us clear of the scene. They obviously didn't know what to do with us themselves – what to tell us, what not to tell us. Maybe they were worried that if they explained to us what had happened they would do it in the wrong way and cause us even more trauma, so they chose to do nothing, to try to ignore the fact that we were there at all, leaving us in a frightening state of limbo.

Someone asked us if we had any relatives they could contact for us and I felt a stab of panic. That was the question police asked when someone had died.

'There are only our godparents,' I said, giving them Helen and Steve's telephone number. 'We don't know any of our relatives.'

After what seemed like an age someone must have come up with the idea of escorting us across the street to the home of a neighbour who lived directly opposite; it was a family who had children at the same school as us, although we didn't know them very well. I think the parents were teachers, like Mum. Their children were sent off upstairs out of the way and we sat down in their living room, where we were left to stare out the window across the street at all the activity going on around our home. It felt as if we were watching a movie about someone else's life, as if it was nothing to do with us.

'What happened?' I asked Alex after everyone else had left us alone.

'There was just one policeman when I got here,' he explained. 'He wouldn't let me go in, then Dad answered the door and the policeman reported a "blue murder" – at least I think that's what he said – and everything went mad after that. They took Dad off in a police car. He wanted to say something to me but they wouldn't let him.'

It was then I realised it must have been Dad I saw being driven away as I came down the street.

'Why was Mum back home early?' I asked, as much to myself as to Alex. 'She didn't say she would be. She would have said. She would have told me she would be able to drive me to my piano lesson. Why was she there?'

He shrugged. He'd told me everything he knew. Alex's isn't one to gabble on if he doesn't have anything constructive or useful to say. We both sank back into our own thoughts.

'What does blue murder mean?' I asked after a minute, but he had no more idea than I did. Then I said out loud the awful words that had formed in my brain. 'Do you suppose he's killed her?'

Alex just stared at me. We were both in a state of shock and neither of us could take anything in but the idea wasn't so preposterous that we could dismiss it out of hand. In a way I think I already knew that Mum was dead, or at least in a critical condition. But if that was so, why wasn't anyone talking to us about it?

Someone came in and told us to stay away from the window. It was yet another thing that didn't make sense at the time but, looking back, I suppose that was the moment when they brought out Mum's body and they didn't want us watching.

It was nearly an hour before the family liaison officer was eventually found and brought into the neighbour's living room to see us. I immediately started firing questions at her, pouring out my anxieties and frustrations, but she told me she would rather wait until our godparents arrived before she answered. There was no changing her mind, so we all sat together in that room, watching the continuing scenes outside, waiting for

Helen to arrive. Gradually the street started to clear as the ambulances and some of the police cars left. Our house had been cordoned off with police tape and secured as a crime scene. It was obvious that nothing further was likely to happen that would require quite so many people in attendance. It was as though the dust was settling, leaving us staring silently at the ruins of our life, still with no real idea what had happened, waiting to be told what we were supposed to do next. I know it sounds crazy but all I could think was that I should have been at my piano lesson. I fretted about whether I should call my piano teacher but I didn't have her number with me.

When Helen arrived she had brought a friend with her; apparently they had been out walking their dogs together when the call from the police came through. We didn't have the sort of relationship with her where she would have hugged us, so she just sat down on the sofa beside us and told us as much as the police had told her.

'He's finally done it,' she said, or at least that was what I heard in my confused state.

'Done it?'

She nodded and I assumed she meant that Dad had attacked Mum but I still couldn't be sure whether she was dead or not. Maybe I was blocking out her words, or maybe Helen just assumed I would understand that was what she meant. She said more but I can't remember anything else about the conversation and neither can Alex.

99

There was no air of surprise in the room – more like a feeling of resignation. It seemed as though we had all been expecting something like this to happen sooner or later. There had been so many threats and so many years of hatred and anger. No one cried. We just sat silent and numb, trying to let the news soak in, not knowing what to say, what the appropriate reaction might be. Helen had a word with the family protection officer who had turned up and then told us that she would take us back to her house. That didn't surprise us either. Mum had always said we would go to Helen and Steve if anything happened to her. I had imagined she meant if she committed suicide or if the cancer got her, not this. Now, it seemed, the moment had come for everything in our lives to change.

Helen's car was parked in the road and as we came outside into the cold evening air my only thought was that I wanted to get inside our house to see what was going on for myself. It didn't seem right that we weren't involved in whatever was happening to our own mother, that these strangers were taking over our lives and just shipping us out. All our lives we had lived there. All our possessions were in there, and our mother had either just died there or been seriously attacked. I wanted to see for myself what had happened. I said nothing and bided my time, my eyes darting around as I tried to work out the best way to get away from the adults surrounding us. As we got close to the car I broke free and made a dash across the road. I didn't really have a plan but I knew that once I was in Helen's car I wouldn't get another chance. But the policemen who had been left to guard the house were ready for me and there was no way I was getting past them, however hard I struggled or however loudly I shouted at them.

There must have been a lot of blood splattered around inside and they were determined I shouldn't disturb the crime scene. Someone took a firm hold of my arm and helped me into the back of the car next to Alex, locking the doors so I couldn't clamber back out before we had driven away. I was shouting at them to let me go. I felt furious at having my life taken over by other people, but I didn't know what I could do about it. Although I was capable for my age in many ways, I was still only fifteen, and I had Alex to think about as well. Mum had always said she knew I would be able to look after him if she went away, so that was what I must do before anything else. I had to make sure they didn't separate us. We only had each other left now.

Chapter Nine

Alex

The family protection officers followed us to our godparents' house and had a quick chat with us before going home for the night. Among other things, they explained to us that we would need to talk to the police the following day. It's difficult to be sure what else they told us and didn't tell us that evening because I suppose we were in a state of shock. It felt as though I was anaesthetised somehow and events were taking place somewhere far away. All the usual patterns and routines of our lives had suddenly been turned upside down and we were having trouble working out what had happened and what was going to happen next. I had thought I knew exactly what I was going to be doing all weekend, and now everything had changed.

Helen did her best to make it seem as though we were a couple of normal guests who had come to stay the night. She concentrated on the domestic details of who was going to sleep where and what we might like to eat for supper, which helped to fill the silence left by our inability to understand what was expected of us. In the end I was allocated a bunk bed in their youngest son's room and their daughter went to stay with a friend so Isobel could use her room. Helen and Steve were quite well off by that stage, always having worked hard at good jobs. They had four children – three boys and a girl – of whom the oldest was already at university. The house had a very different feel to ours, bigger and more comfortable. It had five bedrooms and was located in a much nicer area but we would still rather have been in our own home, even with Dad lurking upstairs in his bedroom. Uncertainty is an uncomfortable emotion.

Even though we hadn't asked for anything, a doctor came round later and tried to persuade us to take some sleeping pills, but we didn't think we needed them. We'd never liked taking anything like that, and the way he was describing them it sounded as though they were going to be ridiculously strong and not very good for you. We didn't want to be knocked out for the whole of the next day when we needed to try to understand what was going on around us. It felt as though every aspect of our lives was being taken over by strangers and we wanted to make sure we were alert enough to let them know what we did and didn't want to do, and to understand fully what had happened to Mum. I remember I just wanted to stay close to Isobel; I felt safer when she was nearby.

Because we hadn't been allowed into our house we only had the clothes we were standing up in and the few bits and pieces we had brought home from school in our bags. Helen rummaged around in her wardrobes and found some of her son's clothes for me (which was a slight problem as I was about four inches taller than him), but the only things in the house for Isobel to wear were very girlie and Isobel always preferred to dress like a tomboy. Horrified by the frilly pink items she was being offered, she rang one of her friends to ask if she could borrow some more comfortable stuff from her.

I can't remember how I slept that night, so I guess it must have been okay even without the tablets. We were probably completely exhausted by everything that had happened in the previous few hours. If I did lie awake at all it was because I was trying to work out what was going on. The whole evening had been so puzzling. The fact that Helen had been so calm and matter of fact had rubbed off on us, or maybe it was the other way round. I knew that Dad had killed Mum. Everyone had been talking in euphemisms so it had been impossible to work out exactly what they were saying, but that phrase 'blue murder' kept ringing in my head.

I hoped that things would be made clearer the next day, and at least we had the weekend to sort ourselves out before we had to be back in school and trying to concentrate on work. I think I was aware that a thing called a 'care system' existed to look after children who couldn't stay with their parents for whatever reason, but I didn't think for a minute that we would end up there. If Mum really wasn't going to be able to look after us, and if Dad was kept in police custody, I assumed we would stay with Helen and Steve. That was what Mum had always said would happen and it seemed like the obvious solution. If this was going to be our new home we might as well get used to it.

The next day Helen went to the police station to be interviewed first of all, then she came back to collect Isobel and me so we could do our interviews. We were taken to a room in a family protection unit that was furnished like a house rather than a police station, with a sofa for us to sit on. Isobel was interviewed first and I went in after. Only one woman asked the questions, but the session was being filmed and we were being watched by CID officers on monitors in the next room. The woman seemed to be trying to find out what we knew about Mum and Dad's relationship and to ascertain what family life had been like up till whatever had happened between them the previous day.

Initially I wasn't particularly interested in co-operating with them. I felt that whatever had happened was the police's fault because they hadn't done anything on the occasions when Isobel had called them out when Dad was beating Mum up. Isobel, in her usual plain-speaking way, actually told them she blamed them. They were really good at calming her down, explaining that when it comes to incidents of domestic abuse they aren't legally able to do anything unless the victim makes an allegation and lodges a complaint. Mum would never have done that; she would never have wanted to bring other people into her problems if she didn't have to, especially the police. They were good at putting us at our ease and winning us over to their side.

Neither of us found the experience too traumatic once we had settled down and realised the woman interviewing us was willing to joke about a bit. We were still having trouble working out what had happened and the real seriousness of it all hadn't sunk in. I don't think we actually knew how we felt about anything. Perhaps we were a bit numb from the shock; I certainly felt an air of unreality about everything. In a way it felt quite therapeutic to talk openly about what it had been like to live in our house after so many years of guarding Mum's privacy and pretending to the outside world that everything was okay.

The police told us later they were surprised by how relaxed we were that day. I guess they expected us to be more shocked that our own father could do such a thing, but all our lives we had been listening to him issuing threats of one sort or another. We had seen him hitting Mum and Alfie, and we always knew he was consumed with hatred for the world and capable of terrible violence. Perhaps it had always been at the back of our minds that something like this could happen, although we had told ourselves that he would never go that far. Mum's cancer had also prepared us a little for the possibility that she might die. Obviously if we had thought it was likely he would do something as drastic as murdering her we would have tried to persuade Mum to leave him and take us with her, but whatever he had done the day before hadn't changed our feelings towards him. We had always hated him and the way he treated us. He had simply proved that we were right in our assessment of him.

The officers were quite good at making us feel relaxed and comfortable. Isobel says she started giggling when she was asked my full name, because she and Mum used to have a joke between them that it was 'Alexandra'. It didn't occur to her that it might have appeared odd to be laughing at a time like that. Because we still had each other we automatically felt less vulnerable than other children might have done in that situation. Isobel had always been the most important person in my life, and as long as she was there I knew I would be OK. I knew she would always protect me.

I gleaned more information about what had happened when the woman told me that Dad had attacked Mum with a 'sharpened chisel'.

'Did you ever see him sharpening a chisel?' she asked me.

I guess if I'd been able to say that I had, they thought they would stand a better chance of proving that the murder was premeditated. They wanted to know whether he had become annoyed by Mum that day and gone and sharpened it with the intention of attacking her, or whether he had been planning it for ages.

'I think that chisel was mine at some point,' I told them when they showed me a picture of it. 'I know it was in my room on Friday morning because Dad had been using it to fix in a new phone point. I don't know anything about it being sharpened though.'

I knew they were videoing everything we said, but I don't think I realised it would all one day be played out in court in front of Dad and the judge and jury and anyone else who might have turned up. I expect they told me but I wasn't really taking much in at that stage.

It was a bit like being presented with a puzzle to solve, like watching a whodunnit on television. Why Dad would have sharpened the chisel at all was a mystery to Isobel and me as well as to the police. There were plenty of knives in the house and dozens of other potential weapons in the garage, from hammers to iron bars, none of which would need customising for the job. If he had preplanned the murder, why didn't he just leave one of these somewhere handy?

Helen gave the police a lot of information that weekend as well. Although she was doing a good job of keeping up a normal façade around us, we realised later when we saw her tapes played back in court how deeply upset she was by the death of her friend. She knew more about what Mum had been living through than anyone else and she let her anger towards Dad spill out to the police in her statement, forgetting that before long she would have to go through the whole thing again, in court, in front of him.

Both Isobel and I owned mobile phones but we had left them inside the house the previous morning, since we weren't allowed to take them to school with us, and the police made it clear there was no way they were going to let us go back for them. Having seen how quick they had been to stop Isobel going anywhere near the front door, we knew they meant it. It was hard to make contact with our friends over the weekend except for the ones whose numbers we knew by heart. I managed to get hold of some of my mates, and when others went to the house the policemen guarding it told them where we had gone. They then came round to visit us with a 'trick or treat' box of sweets and magazines and funny photographs to cheer us up. It was a brilliant gesture that I really appreciated.

By Sunday morning we were able to read all about what Dad had done to Mum on the front page of the local papers. Even though we were both underage the paper openly printed our names and ages, our school and our home address, with pictures of the house in case anyone was still in doubt. Apparently it had been on the television and radio news broadcasts throughout Saturday as well but we hadn't heard any of them, so we found out most of the details about how our mother had died from the newspapers. Helen had to agree to let us read the story because we would otherwise have heard people talking about it at school.

Whereas everyone else seemed keen to avoid telling us anything face to face for fear of upsetting us, the local reporters had no such qualms. Dad, they informed us, had stabbed Mum 'between fifty and sixty times' in the head and upper body with the 'sharpened chisel' that the police had been asking us about. The attack had been so frenzied and ferocious that the forensics people couldn't tell exactly how many times he had struck, but the force of his blows had chipped bones and penetrated her breastplate. I felt sick to my stomach reading it, trying to imagine the terror Mum must have been experiencing during his onslaught. The pain must have been unbelievable. I didn't say anything with Helen in the room but I cried later for the first time since it happened when Isobel and I were on our own. The details were just so horrific. How hard do you have to hit someone to penetrate their bones?

no one listened

The police weren't happy about our names being published in the press and after they complained to the editor they were withdrawn, but it was too late by then. The papers had been printed and distributed, everyone who had ever known us or ever known anyone who had known us, could read all about it. Complete strangers who had never heard of us before now knew exactly who we were and where they could find us. From then on, in all their future stories, the reporters referred to us as 'the children who cannot be named for legal reasons'. Talk about shutting the stable door after the horse has bolted!

We kept asking the adults who seemed to have taken over our lives if we could go to school as normal on Monday morning. We both wanted to have the comfort of our familiar routine and it was awkward being in someone else's house all the time, even when it was people we knew as well as Helen and Steve's family. We didn't know what to do with all the hours in the day to distract ourselves from thinking about Mum and we wanted to be back amongst our friends and filling our minds with other distractions. But the school authorities said we had to stay away for a day because they wanted to make an official announcement about it at assembly first and they thought it would be difficult for us if we were there. Because we had been mentioned in the paper they thought it was appropriate to tell eleven hundred other people, most of whom had had no idea who we were until that moment, all the intimate details of our family tragedy. The idea struck us as a bit strange but they were adamant that it was the right way to handle things and we were left sitting around the house for another day, wondering what would happen to us next.

When they made the announcement to the whole school, they also said that if any of our friends felt too traumatised by the news they should come forward and they would be offered support. We couldn't quite understand why they thought anyone else would need any support. A few of our friends knew Mum because of our activities, but virtually none of them had ever met Dad. No one was offering any counselling to Isobel and me, so why would they offer it to other people?

Anyone at our school who hadn't seen it on the news or read about it in the papers got to hear about Mum's murder at assembly on Monday morning. We were told later that some of the teachers were actually crying during the announcement, as though they had lost a close friend or their own mother. Maybe they were crying for us rather than for Mum but I'd only been at the school for one term by then so none of them knew me particularly well. I guess they thought they could imagine how it might feel to suddenly find yourself with no home and no parents. The only thing was, Isobel and I weren't sure how we felt. The main sensation was still a sense of numbness and unreality, combined with a niggling anxiety about what would become of us now. I couldn't let myself think about missing Mum. Maybe I was too scared of what might come out if I opened the floodgates. We'd been brought up learning to keep control of our emotions and it seemed safest to continue doing so now for as long as I could.

Many years later, when I read the reports of psychologists who interviewed us in the months after Mum's death, I learned that they thought we were suffering from 'dissociation', which is a side effect of post-traumatic stress disorder. The feeling of emotional detachment we both experienced in the early days was a symptom of the way our brains were trying to protect us from the sheer horror of what we'd been through. It's a phenomenon that is fairly common following huge trauma, and it's something that would continue to affect us in different ways for years to come, making it difficult for us to trust anyone apart from each other. At that stage I just felt that I was watching a movie of events that I wasn't really part of.

Chapter Ten

Isobel

On the Tuesday they let us go back to school, which was a relief to me because I had a running competition that I didn't want to miss that afternoon. It might sound strange, but Alex and I were craving distractions from what had happened and if there was one thing Mum had always drilled into us it was that there was no excuse for missing commitments and letting other people down. We had never been allowed to take days off sick unless we were completely incapable of walking, and we knew that she would never have allowed us to use her death as an excuse to give up on the things that she had worked so hard to help us achieve. Working hard at school and never letting other people down in out-of-school activities were the most important things in the world to her; more important than having a happy or harmonious home, more important than her own peace of mind, in the end maybe even more important than her own life. We didn't know any other way to behave. Mum

had never made a fuss about anything in her life, so why
would we? To be honest, we wouldn't even have known
how to begin.

I took after Mum in a lot of ways, one of which was a
ferociously competitive streak. If I was beaten by anyone
else in an exam or a race I would become really frustrated and cross with myself. I think that determination
to be the best at everything helped to keep me going
through those early, confusing and difficult days after the
murder, powering my feet through the school gates
when most other people would have stayed home and
concentrated on trying to straighten out their heads and
their emotional lives. I just decided to grit my teeth and
get on with things.

The first time we walked into school together after
the announcement in assembly, Alex and I could see
people were staring at us, which felt strange. We had
never been the sort of kids who wanted to draw attention
to themselves. It was a bit as though we'd become acci-
dental celebrities. Everyone knew who we were, even if
we didn't always know who they were. I suppose that is
what life is like for people who appear on television regularly. Random people we didn't know very well would
come up to us with concerned expressions on their faces
and ask if we were okay. It felt as though they wanted to
be close to us just because our family had been in the
papers, as if that made us interesting or exciting in some

way and they hoped some of it would rub off on them. Some people seemed to like the idea of being involved in anything even remotely notorious.

People have remarked since that Alex and I were very quiet and withdrawn during this period. I suppose they expected us to break down and sob, but it didn't work like that. We had our moments but we kept them private, just between ourselves. In fact, we were more dazed than anything else, trying to sort out our thoughts and feelings, while at the same time trying to keep up with our schoolwork and not be too much of a burden to Helen and Steve. I remember wandering from one lesson to the next that first day, sitting down and hearing the teacher's words washing over me but not being able to focus for long enough on what they were saying to be able to make sense of it or remember anything. My concentration kept wandering off into a sort of no-man's land. It was like living in limbo. My mind was trying to take so much in, trying to sort it and make sense of it. We still didn't really know what had happened on the previous Friday because a lot of what had appeared in the papers had been speculation. How, for instance, had that first policeman known to turn up on the doorstep when he did? Why had Mum come home early from school? What had made Dad finally erupt so dramatically after so many years? When would we be able to go back home? What would happen to Dad now? Would we be his next victims? He had never made any secret of the fact that he hated me just as much as he hated Mum, so presumably he would like to see me dead too. I guess he knew we would be at Helen and Steve's and I did have moments of anxiety thinking he might come to get me.

Over the following days the police kept coming back to interview us whenever they thought of something new to ask, but we had no idea what was going on in their investigation beyond the tiny snippets of information they would let slip. Knowing that we were growing bored of going over the same questions time and time again, they started bribing us to co-operate by offering to get things for us from the house, like our mobile phones. It wasn't that we were being uncooperative; we were just tired of talking in circles without reaching any new conclusions and we longed to go back to being quiet, anonymous and private. I think they knew they were putting us under stress by constantly interrupting our school and home routine with their visits and they felt they should do something for us in return.

We were told we'd had a 'guardian ad liteum' assigned to us. I think that is a legal requirement for any children who find themselves in our position. This guardian's main job was to represent our views and our best interests in court if social services applied for a care order. Apparently our care proceedings were deemed to be complicated and so had to be held at a London High

Court rather than a local one, but no one explained any of this to us and our main concerns were about continuing with our daily lives and trying to find a level of normalcy. After school each day we went back home to our godparents' house and continued with all our usual after-school activities, just as we had done when Mum was around. It seemed strange that something so dramatic had happened and so much had changed, yet a percentage of our lives continued more or less as before. It gave us something to cling onto through those traumatic first weeks.

Helen has since told us how surprised she was that neither Alex nor I ever wanted to talk about how we felt and never shed a tear in front of her, but then I never saw her or Steve cry either; they just kept going, even though I know they must have missed Mum almost as much as we did. Like Mum, Helen was a very private woman who didn't like to talk about her feelings, at least not to us.

We saw social workers from time to time, and about a month after Mum died one of them blurted out something about Mum's suicide attempt. Alex hadn't known about this before. I looked at her aghast and thought, 'Oh, thanks very much!' As if poor Alex didn't have enough shocking news to cope, he had the trauma of finding out that Mum had tried to kill herself as well. The woman's lack of tact was unbelievable. Being Alex, he seemed to take it in his stride but I always worry about what goes on beneath the surface with him.

I tried once or twice to get back into our house to retrieve more of my possessions, but whenever I got to the door there was always a policeman standing guard. When they eventually agreed, after a couple of weeks, to let us have some of our own clothes, they still wouldn't allow us back into the house to fetch them ourselves. A policeman was sent in with a list of the things we wanted, but of course he came back with all the wrong stuff.

Gradually we were piecing together more snippets of information about what might have happened that afternoon, although we still couldn't find out the whole truth because Dad was denying he could remember anything. From the moment the police came to the front door he claimed that he didn't recall anything of the incident. His story was that he could remember Mum coming home and he remembered telling her that he was just fixing the phone extension in Alex's room. The next thing he could recall was coming downstairs and finding Mum slumped over the waste bin and another bin in which we kept dog biscuits just near the back door in the kitchen.

'I assumed I must have done something,' he said in his statement, which was later played in court, 'so I rang the police.'

Why would that be his initial assumption if he didn't remember anything? When he saw Mum slumped there, wouldn't his first thought have been that she had fainted or fallen over? Why didn't he go to see what was wrong with her before calling the police? In fact she was lying there with his chisel still sticking out of her from the final blow, so if he had gone to look he would have known exactly what he had done. I felt angry and cheated when I heard he was denying any memory of events. We wanted to know what had happened and felt we had a right to know. Trust him to deny us even that!

We would eventually learn that he made two phone calls to the police that afternoon. The first must have been made just as we were finishing school, while I was searching around the changing rooms for my PE kit and Alex was coming out of his class and getting ready to start his saunter home. We heard recordings of the calls in court and in the first one he told the police clearly that he had killed his wife. I guess he must have expected that an announcement like that would bring them round in force within minutes, but they obviously didn't take the call seriously for some reason. I don't know how many false alarms they get in a day, with people claiming they have committed murders, but there was obviously something about the way he spoke to them which made them doubt he was genuine.

Every minute that he was waiting in the house for the police to arrive must have seemed like an hour as he imagined Alex and me drawing closer and getting out our keys to unlock the front door. After about fifteen minutes his nerve broke and he rang them again.

'My children are due home,' he warned them, 'they're going to be walking through the front door at any moment.'

He must have been able to picture us in the streets outside, getting closer and closer to the house, completely unaware of the scene that would be awaiting us if we weren't stopped. Why did he suddenly care about protecting us? Was he worried we would be traumatised at seeing our mother dead in the kitchen, her blood spattering the walls? He had never cared for a second about traumatising us before. Was he worried that he might attack us as well? Or was he worried we might attack him when we saw what he had done? Why did he not simply deadlock the door so we couldn't get in until the police arrived? Nothing to do with Dad's behaviour ever really made any logical sense and it certainly made no sense at all that afternoon.

Even after the second call the police still couldn't have been taking him very seriously because they only dispatched one man to the scene, and that was the guy who turned up on the doorstep at the same moment as Alex arrived home and put his key in the lock.

As the reality of our bereavement began to sink in, we asked if we could see Mum's body. They told us we would be able to see her after the three post-mortems were over, but then they seemed to forget about it. A month after her death, when preparations for her funeral were under way, we asked again and they said we couldn't see her now because the body had 'decomposed too much', which they thought would be too unsettling for us. I'm sure they could have covered up anything they thought would be too unpleasant for us, but they decided not to. I am also sceptical that she could have decomposed much as I presume the body was frozen or chilled or whatever they do in mortuaries.

Although they didn't intend to let us see her, the police still needed someone to identify the body. Helen and Steve refused to do it but Jillian, Mum's friend from school, agreed, even though she was surprised to be asked, imagining there would be other people from around our area the police would have gone to first.

I think if Alex and I could have seen her dead it would have given us at least a bit of closure. One of the hardest things for us to come to terms with is accepting that we will almost certainly never know what happened to her in the final few minutes of her life. The fact that she just vanished from our lives and the last time we saw her was when she was rushing to get out of the house on time that morning made it seem as though nothing had really ended for us. Seeing the body wouldn't have answered any of the questions that spun round and round in our heads whenever we weren't distracted, but it would still have helped to quieten them. Maybe it would have made everything seem more real. At the very least, I would have liked to stroke her hair one last time and whisper goodbye and that I loved her.

Chapter Eleven

Alex

The police cordons were left round our house even after the last police guard had been withdrawn. Despite the cordons, and despite the story being plastered all over the front pages of the local papers, the newsagent continued to deliver Sunday papers to the doorstep for me to distribute. We only realised that when we saw them stacked up outside on the doorstep in a news picture.

The computer Mum had bought us to help with our homework was taken away so they could check to see if Dad had written anything on it that might help to explain what had been happening between them, or give an insight into his state of mind at the moment when he finally snapped. The only thing they found that interested them was an odd story that Isobel had written about Mum and Dad arguing, which they duly trawled through in minute detail, looking for signs that she was disturbed by whatever had been going on in the family.

After studying it, they decided it just reflected her life. It probably did, but that was because we'd been leading disturbed lives in many ways for years, not because we were actually disturbed ourselves. Mostly we were just angry at the way Dad had treated us all and how he had deliberately sabotaged our family, something he had been trying to do for years before he finally succeeded in destroying everything.

Jillian, Mum's long-time lab assistant, proved to be a great friend to her and to us. Realising that we had been stranded with no money at all with which to pay for Mum to have a funeral, she took a collection at the school. The service was held in our local church about a month after Mum died. I was shocked when I got there to see how packed it was, mostly with people neither Isobel nor I had ever seen before. I think a lot of them must have been Mum's work colleagues; others were probably the parents of children at our school. All these strangers seemed to know who we were as we walked in, which made it even more of a surreal experience. The funeral directors must have announced that it was happening in the paper because Helen had warned us that the press might be there, looking for a follow-up story. Although I don't think they did turn up in the end there was so much happening that was beyond our understanding they may well have been there and we didn't notice them.

The organisers had asked us what songs we wanted sung at the service and whether we would like to say anything ourselves, a tribute to Mum. Neither of us fancied standing up in front of so many strangers and letting them into any more of our family secrets than they'd already been privy to through the media. In the end the head teacher from Mum's school agreed to speak about her, which was kind.

'Make sure you cry,' Helen whispered to Isobel as we walked through the crowd to our seats in the front row, but neither of us did. Not then, not in public. Helen must have thought it would reflect badly on us if we were seen to be coping too well. Not breaking down might have made us look heartless but that was never the way we did things. We were like Mum in that way. Even though it had been a month since the death, the sense of complete unreality and confusion prevailed. Everything felt as though it was completely out of our hands. No one really explained anything to us in words that we could understand. It was as if they didn't want to upset us so they just avoided talking about the subject that was uppermost in all our minds. Even as we walked into the church and took our seats we had no idea what would happen during the ceremony because neither of us had ever been to a funeral before, and we had even less idea what was going to happen afterwards.

Both of us found it hard to cry. Right from the beginning Dad had drummed it into us that we mustn't, that it was wimpish. When he and Mum were having their terrible fights and he was screaming and shouting at us, he would become even angrier if he saw tears welling up in our eyes.

'Don't cry!' he would yell and we would be frightened into straight-faced silence. After a while it became a habit. I don't remember ever seeing Mum cry and we tended to be practical about things anyway, just like her. I remember her falling over on an icy pavement once and cracking her head open badly. I could tell she was in real pain but still she didn't cry. It wasn't till Helen came round and told her that she really needed to get some stitches that she agreed to go to the hospital. It turned out she needed about twenty stitches.

I had a similar experience when I was with Isobel and her friend at the local swings one day. They were playing that game where you go really high and then jump off mid-swing and I wanted to copy them. Eventually they agreed to give me a turn but I was too small to pull it off and fell awkwardly, all my weight landing on my wrist. I didn't cry so they picked me up and dusted me off before going swimming together while I went home to play on my PlayStation. My arm really hurt but I didn't want to make a fuss because I assumed it would get better. By the time Isobel got back from swimming about two hours later I was in bed and my arm had turned black. Mum decided I had better go to the hospital and when the doctors investigated they discovered it was severely broken. I don't believe I shed a single tear through the whole event.

I think if small children never get fussed over when they cry, and maybe even get shouted at or worse, they soon learn that it's not worth doing and give up. You sometimes see pictures on television from orphanages in places like Eastern Europe where the children have been terribly neglected or abused and you very seldom hear them crying. They give up bothering because it never does them any good. Mum wasn't very demonstrative physically, rarely giving us cuddles, but it didn't matter because we were never in any doubt that she loved us. She dedicated her whole life to bringing us up as well as she possibly could, so it never occurred to us to worry about the fact that she wasn't physically affectionate.

We taught ourselves to distance our thoughts from our feelings even further as the years went by. If we hadn't done that we would have been sobbing all the time after Mum died and everything in our lives would have ground to a halt at that moment, probably including our education. We couldn't allow that to happen because that would have been a victory for Dad, who always wanted to show Mum that she was wasting her time with all the things she did for us. We cried quiet, private tears when we were on our own, but our main goal was to just get on with things as best we could.

Helen asked us whether Mum would have wanted to be buried or cremated, but we had no idea.

'What about your grandparents?' she asked. 'Were they cremated?'

We had no idea about that either. We thought cremation was probably the best idea, considering the state Mum's body was going to be in after the murder and the post mortem. Personally, I wasn't quite sure what happened at a cremation and it wasn't until a social worker, who we had never met before, told us at the end of the twenty-minute funeral service at the church that the cremation would follow next that I found out.

'Your godparents don't want to go to the crematorium,' she told us. 'Do you want to go?'

'Yes,' Isobel said firmly.

Both of us wanted to stay with Mum till the very last minute. It didn't seem right to send her off wherever she was going on her own. It was over half an hour's drive to the crematorium. We sat in a black car, following behind the hearse that held her coffin. No one else came on from the church, so it was just Isobel and me and two social workers who had never met Mum, who were there to witness her body departing on its final journey. I stared and stared at that coffin throughout the short ceremony at the crematorium, trying to picture Mum's body inside and wondering what it looked like now. Somehow it was hard to believe that she was in there. When a curtain came across and we heard the trundling sound of her coffin heading down to the furnace, I had a huge lump in my throat and tightness in my chest. I just gripped Isobel's hand as hard as I could to keep control.

The social workers took us back to the church again but everyone else had left by that stage. We found out later that some cousins of Mum's had been there for the service, but they didn't introduce themselves to us so we didn't even find out that they existed until later.

Jillian had put together a book of condolences, full of letters from people who had worked with Mum for years, talking about what an inspiring and dedicated teacher she was, and how much of herself she gave up to help her pupils. The letters were all full of praise for her vivacity and the way in which she brought her subjects to life when she taught; they talked about how she would jump around the classroom, animating otherwise dry topics, always happy and hyperactive. I know you expect people to be polite and say nice things after someone has died, but these letters seemed far more sincere and enthusiastic and affectionate than you would have expected. It was a strange feeling to read about our mother as if she was a completely different person to the woman who lived such a difficult life at home. In the last year or two of her life she had seemed so weary and run down and defeated when she was with us, but she must have come alive the moment she arrived at that school in a way she never could when she was at home and living under Dad's ominous shadow. By the time she got back to us in the evening she would have been working or driving for about twelve hours and what was left of her energy had been drained out of her.

One of the letters talked about how keen Mum had always been for girls to take their education seriously. 'She was passionate about getting girls to believe in themselves and use their abilities to their greatest advantage,' it read. That was definitely what she believed for herself and for Isobel, and she was equally determined that I should be given every possible educational opportunity that she could manage to provide, even though she sometimes doubted I would take as much advantage of my intelligence as I was capable of doing. There were times when teachers had trouble holding my attention.

It was very moving for us to read about the effect she'd had on other people's lives, people we knew nothing about, reminding us that she had lived a whole other life away from the unhappiness and drudgery of her marriage. Away from Dad's vindictive influence she was seen as someone special rather than someone despicable and hated. It made us appreciate even more just how much she had done for us over the years.

Jillian was our only link with Mum's past. She loved to talk about their early days together, and it was her who told us about the time Mum invited her and a few other colleagues to our house for supper and Dad came into the room stark naked. I don't think Mum ever invited anyone back to the house again after that, which was probably exactly the result that he had wanted to achieve. She kept in touch with us, sending Christmas and birthday presents every year. Even now, whenever we make contact with her she is always keen to know every detail of what has been going on in our lives and to support us in any way she can.

But Jillian was just a good woman and a kind friend. She didn't have any real responsibility for us. She didn't really know us at all. She lived miles away and had her own life to lead. Our life now was with Helen and Steve and we began to get used to it, falling into comfortable routines very similar to the ones we had always followed. Initially Alfie had been put into kennels while everyone worked out what to do with him, but Isobel and I kept pleading for him and eventually Helen weakened and let us bring him to their home. She had been reluctant initially because they had two dogs of their own, which they didn't want to upset. As usual it was poor old Alfie who got bullied because their dogs became fiercely territorial and wouldn't let him eat his meals. We were still happy to have him back, something of our old familiar lives returned to us, and we hoped he would settle down eventually.

No one ever suggested for a moment that we should go anywhere else, so we assumed that was going to be our home until we left school. Mum had always said Helen and Steve would look after us if anything happened to her, so Isobel and I didn't give the matter any more thought. All we cared about was that we should be together and should have Alfie with us, and we tried to be as little trouble as possible. We just needed somewhere to do our homework and sleep after school and someone to help us get around to our various activities for a couple of years until Isobel was old enough to drive. Helen and Steve were taking over from Mum; that was what we told anyone who asked. We assured everyone we would be okay as long as we could stay together.

Our school lives and activities were continuing as normal and although it was awkward being a permanent guest in someone else's house, particularly when there was so much going on in everyone's heads that was being left unsaid, we were starting to think of it as our home. We knew that there had been a social worker visiting the house and we had seen her briefly, but no one explained why she was there or what her duties were towards us.

'Do you have any relatives?' this woman asked us one day, about six weeks after Mum died. 'Anyone you might be able to live with?'

She took us completely by surprise. Weren't we going to live with Helen and Steve then?

'No,' we explained, 'nobody. We never met Dad's family. We don't even know their names. And Mum was an only child. Our grandparents are both dead.'

Isobel vaguely remembered some relative of Mum's writing her a newsletter one Christmas, but she had no more information than that, apart from describing where she thought the letter might be. The social worker must have got permission from the police to go into the house because she found the letter and the woman turned out to be a cousin of Mum's. We eventually found out she had three cousins, all of whom had been receiving regular updates about us from Mum all through our lives. She had never mentioned them to us as far as we can remember. We can only think that Mum didn't want too much contact with any of her relatives in case they came to visit and met Dad. Or maybe, like Jillian, they had come to the house and Dad had made it very clear that he didn't want them to come back. It was better for her to keep everyone separate and at a distance from one another than to risk the embarrassment of Dad behaving threateningly and embarrassing her.

Towards the end of February the social worker who had been assigned to us arrived at the house and told us that some people were going to be coming in a couple of hours who wanted to meet us. No one explained exactly why they were coming, but Isobel and I realised that everything was about to change again.

The couple were a lot older than Mum and Dad. They were both overweight, the man only a bit over five feet tall but weighing nearly twenty stone. The woman was taller than him, but she must have been around sixteen stone. They introduced themselves to us but we were both in such a state of confusion and panic that their names went in one ear and out the other. We didn't feel that we could ask them to tell us again, so we just kept quiet and waited, hoping someone would call them by their names and give us a clue. No one did, so the awkwardness continued.

I wasn't really concentrating on the conversations going on around us. I had no idea who they were or what they had to do with us, but I did notice they were telling us about their home as if they were trying to convince us how much we would like it, and it started to dawn on me that we might be going to live with them. No one had even mentioned 'fostering' up till then. I'm not sure I would have known what the word meant. Neither Helen nor Steve had said anything about what would happen to us next, or so much as hinted that we might not be staying with them. We were completely dumb-struck, unable to understand what was going on, unable even to think how to phrase the many questions that were circling round inside our heads.

The visitors asked us what we thought of them, which was an impossible question to answer so we just shrugged and laughed nervously. It was at that stage that we realised they were planning to pack our things and take us with them there and then. They were even agreeing to take Alfie as well, which we later discovered was an unusual thing for a foster family to agree to.

'Will we be able to go to the same school, and keep up all our after-school activities?' I asked, and they agreed that we would. We explained that we would need to be driven to different venues virtually every night of the week and they smiled and agreed that that was absolutely fine.

Isobel and I didn't know what to say after that but we asked for a little time to think about it all and get used to the idea, and this was agreed.

For some strange reason, things kept happening to us on the eleventh of each month. Mum had been killed on the 11th of January and her funeral was held on the 11th of February. On the 11th of March, two weeks after we were first introduced to them, and still not able to remember what they had said their names were, we found ourselves in a car being driven to our new home with our new foster parents.

To this day Helen has never explained to us when she made the decision that we couldn't stay with her, or whether she had never intended it to happen in the first place. I suppose from their perspective they may never have expected to take us on full time. We arrived at a moment when they were shocked and grieving over Mum's death as well. I can see that it is hard to have two new people suddenly arriving in your family without warning, and the sleeping arrangements had been a bit cramped with us and the other three children who still lived at home. It just seemed strange that no one ever explained to us what was being planned for us. Maybe everyone assumed someone else had told us. Isobel and I still feel anger towards Helen when we think back on it. I would certainly behave differently if the children of a friend of mine were orphaned. I'm pretty sure I would have a bit more humanity.

Chapter Twelve

Isobel

We drove for about twenty minutes from Helen and Steve's house, leaving Redditch behind us and heading towards Evesham, some ten miles away. We had no idea where we were going and didn't feel that we could really ask. I was beginning to wonder how we would be able to get back to our school and our activities if we ended up living too far away. Had anyone thought that through? As soon as they had seen us into the house Helen and our social worker left, hardly even stopping to say goodbye after they had handed us over to our new foster parents. We didn't hear from Helen again for a good few months after that, which felt strange because we had seen her almost every day when we'd lived in Redditch, even before we moved in with them. One by one, it seemed, the familiar faces from our former lives were vanishing and being replaced by strangers.

We assumed that Helen didn't come round because she was giving us time to settle in but later she told me that she stayed away because she thought the foster parents were 'weird' and she 'got a bad vibe off the man'. I was pretty shocked when she said that. Surely that was all the more reason to pop back now and then to check that we were all right? I suppose everyone has their own way of dealing with grief. The foster parents had their own social worker, and she was there when we arrived at our new home.

The house was very similar to the one we had been born and brought up in, although they would soon be doing lots of work to extend it at the back. We each had our own bedrooms. There was also a front room that they didn't use very much and Alex and I pretty much colonised it from day one as our own private space and sanctuary. We didn't know what was expected of us or how we should interact with these people whose house and lives we had suddenly been thrust into. We didn't want to get in their way and so we would disappear into the front room together and close the door until it was time to do something specific like eat a meal or go to bed, talking to each other all the time, keeping ourselves separate.

We'd been there about two weeks before we found out that our foster parents' names were Cathy and Pete. It must have made us seem really rude because we were just saying 'oi' if we wanted to attract their attention, too embarrassed to ask after so long. Eventually the penny must have dropped.

'We've noticed,' the woman said, 'that you never use our names. Do you actually know what they are?'

There was no point lying. I think, because we were the first foster kids they had had, they were as much at sea about how to deal with the situation as we were. They had been on holiday the week before they took us on, so the social workers hadn't been able to brief them as thoroughly as they might have done on our background. As a result, they had found out most of the details of our situation from newspaper articles on the Internet, which gave our family history a very negative spin, suggesting that we were all horribly dysfunctional. Cathy kept trying to quiz us about our background in the early days, asking loads of personal questions that we didn't want to answer. I suppose our reluctance to open up was disappointing to them, and may even have seemed rude, but it's just the way we were. As far as we were concerned they were strangers and we wouldn't have dreamed of telling them all about life at home with Mum and Dad just to satisfy their curiosity.

Both of them liked to drink and would consume several bottles of wine between them during the course of an evening. It was a puzzle to us how they had passed the tests needed to be accepted as foster parents, but maybe the authorities had become desperate when they realised our godparents had no desire to keep us, and couldn't find anyone more suitable who was willing to take on two potentially traumatised teenagers and a dog. They had each had children themselves, although not together, and their children were all grown up by then, with their own families. Some of them came to meet us soon after we arrived, but they didn't seem to want to get involved in their parents' latest 'scheme'. It felt as though we were being paraded in front of even more people we didn't know and we couldn't think of a thing to say, so we probably struck them as two pretty dull children.

If the grandchildren were staying at the house we would be used as a baby-sitting service once Cathy and Pete had started drinking in the evening, or if they were throwing a dinner party and didn't want to be disturbed. We used to be able to hear them talking to their friends about us in the dining room, as if we were an interesting case study, which I suppose is pretty much what we were to them. Their guests never came through to introduce themselves though. Maybe we gave off a hostile vibe, but I don't think so. We were just quiet, as always. People who were told our story but didn't actually talk to us themselves must have been left with the impression that we were troubled children from a dysfunctional background, but that wasn't how we felt. We thought we were getting on with our lives reasonably well; we just weren't sure how to ask for the help we needed in order to do better, help that we had grown so used to receiving unconditionally from Mum.

Their drinking didn't usually make Cathy and Pete unpleasant or aggressive, as it used to make Dad, but it did mean that if we talked to them about anything during the evening they would quite often have forgotten about it by the next day. We relied on them a lot to give us lifts to and from our activities, even more than Mum and Helen because of the distances now involved, but they would often forget we had asked them, or would complain that they weren't able to have a drink because of having to drive. Gradually we had to give up our out-of-school activities just because we could no longer be relied upon to get there as regularly as we once had. It made us appreciate even more how reliable Mum had been all those years. Their promises to do all they could to help us keep up our activities went by the wayside quite quickly; it was soon obvious they had underestimated just how much effort would be involved. I think a lot of people underestimate how much effort it takes to be as conscientious a parent as Mum was to us.

'It's so far,' they would complain. 'Can't you join clubs that are more local?'

Of course we could have done that, but then we would have lost all the friends we had made over the years and we would have had no shared history with our new teammates. We would have been cast even further adrift from our past. We already felt isolated by moving so far away, and losing those ties was cutting us even further adrift from our friends and from our past. In the end, however, Cathy and Pete made us feel so guilty about inconveniencing them that it was easier just to give in and stop asking for lifts. Neither of us felt like going out and starting again at new clubs just yet, especially now it took us so much longer to get back and forth to school each day. Within a month of being with them we weren't doing any extra activities at all. We would just go to school in the morning and come back in the afternoon, do our homework and then sit together in the front room, waiting for bedtime.

We thought about contacting our social worker to try to explain how we felt, but we didn't know how to do that. If we asked Cathy and Pete they immediately demanded to know why we wanted to contact her, as if we were planning to report them for not doing their job properly. We never wanted to upset them unnecessarily, so we kept quiet and concentrated all our efforts on our schoolwork instead. They did drive us to and from school, because the bus routes took too long, but they grumbled a lot about that too, even though they'd known from the start that we wanted to stay at the same school. They wanted us to love and respect them as if they were our real parents, but they didn't actually want to make all the sacrifices that a real mother like Mum has to make.

'Why don't you spend more time with us?' they wanted to know. 'Why do you always shut yourselves away in the front room? You're always talking to each other but you never talk to us. We're all one family now.'

When the question was put to us as bluntly as that it was hard to find an answer. We had just been following our instincts, huddling together for comfort and mutual support because that was what we had always done. It had always been Alex and me against the world. We'd had Mum on our team, of course, and Alfie, and our friends at school, but the most constant elements for both of us were each other. We didn't want to sit watching TV with Cathy and Pete every evening while they guzzled their wine. It was a bonus to us that they had a second front room where we could keep ourselves to ourselves.

I think our new parents would have liked us to tell them our problems, maybe give them a hug now and then and allow them to comfort us when we were sad, but we had never done that with Mum and Dad so we certainly weren't going to start with two virtual strangers. They tried too hard to get to know us, but their questions made me uneasy and I hated it when they were critical of Mum. I became very protective of everything to do with our past. I knew how dysfunctional it had all been, but that didn't mean I wanted other people to tell me it was. I didn't want them judging Mum, or even Dad for that matter. I felt criticisms of them were criticisms of us. It was as if they believed Mum was some sort of bad person for allowing the things that happened

144

to happen. While Cathy and Pete probably believed they were attempting to bond with us, their efforts made us all the more silent and insular as we tried to protect ourselves from criticism.

They kept saying things like: 'I can't get my head round why your Mum didn't just leave him.'

It didn't seem to occur to them that we had already wondered the same thing a million times, and we didn't need to be reminded of it every day by someone who had never even met Mum. How do you explain to someone who thinks completely differently that Mum was both proud and stubborn and didn't want to admit to the outside world that her marriage had failed so catastrophically? She would rather have kept on working at things than give up. The foster parents would never have been able to understand that, even if we had been able to find the words to explain it. Mum's greatest concern was always to keep things even and stable so that Alex and I would have as little disruption to our education as possible.

'We can't understand why you were forced to do so many activities all the time,' was something else they kept saying when they couldn't be bothered to drive us somewhere we wanted to go.

But we were never forced to do anything. Mum might have encouraged us, and she might have got annoyed when we gave things up for no obvious reason, but she had never forced us to take part in any activities. We did them because we enjoyed them, and whenever we stopped enjoying them we gave them up. We resented being judged by these two people who still didn't know us at all. Sometimes it felt as though they were jealous of our past family life and wanted to reconstruct us in their own image as their own children. They wanted us to hate our own family and our own past so much we would be grateful for any love and support they might be offering us now. They couldn't understand how we could still love Mum so much when, to their way of thinking, she had let us down and given us much less than they were willing to give.

Alex was my whole family by that stage and I didn't feel either of us needed anyone else emotionally; we just needed food and a roof over our heads and someone to drive us to school so that we could continue to function in the world and finish our educations. It made for an awkwardness in the relationship with our foster parents that none of us knew how to solve. We didn't feel we knew them enough to trust them with all the personal stuff that was going on in our minds and because we had each other we didn't feel the need to share the pain or confusion with anyone else, particularly two complete strangers. They wanted to look after Alex as if they were his parents and they resented the fact that he didn't need them to do that because he had me. I used to tuck him

146

into bed each night and give him a goodnight kiss and I think they felt that should have been their role, but they were still strangers to us. They wanted to become our family, but we just wanted to get on with them in a civil manner; we weren't looking for a replacement for our real family.

It wasn't as though Cathy and Pete didn't try to do the right things at the beginning. They used to take us out for walks with the dog, for example, but they never took us separately, so we were always talking to each other, deliberately avoiding any attempts they might make to bond with us. Perhaps if they had been more experienced at fostering they would have known better how to win us over individually, breaking down the many barriers we had erected around ourselves. They tried very hard in many ways.

In the morning they would make us enormous cooked breakfasts but we just weren't used to it, always having grabbed bowls of cereal as we got ready for school. They also cooked a lot of hearty meat-based dinners, like spaghetti Bolognese, and I had been vegetarian for years, but I didn't feel I could tell them that at first. When they did find out, they seemed to think it was more evidence that Mum hadn't looked after us properly, and told me that if I wanted food that was different from what they were eating, I would have to cook it myself. I could see that they were hurt by our inability to enjoy

147

their hospitality, but we just couldn't eat as much as they did, and preferred to make simple dishes for ourselves.

From time to time we were visited by psychologists who were preparing reports for a care proceedings court case. One of these interviews took place with our foster parents in the room.

'So what is better about your life now that you're in foster care,' the psychologist asked, 'compared to your old life?'

Alex and I said nothing. We were aware that our silence sounded rude because of everything Cathy and Pete were doing for us, but we didn't want to say anything that was disrespectful to Mum's memory. We weren't willing to be led into saying we hadn't always been happy with her, because it wouldn't have been true.

'We get more pocket money,' Alex said eventually, when the silence had become unbearable, which I guess probably made us sound mercenary and ungrateful.

To begin with, Pete was nicer to us than Cathy. He was a bit like a big, cuddly teddy bear of a man, giving us money and organising holidays and treats, but sometimes things that started out being well-meant ended up creating misunderstandings between us. During that first summer, they took us to visit a friend of theirs who had a speed boat that towed 'doughnut boats' around a lake. We had a fantastic day being pulled around, bumping into each other and falling off into the water, screaming with laughter all the time. By the end of the day our arms were covered in bruises. We had a visit from a social worker a couple of days later and I made a joke about the bruises while our foster parents were in the room. I was trying my best to lighten the atmosphere between us all by making little jokes because Alex was finding it harder and harder to pretend that he liked them and was falling more and more silent during social worker visits.

'Look what they've been doing to us,' I laughed, displaying the black and blue patches, before adding that I was only joking.

Cathy and Pete were utterly mortified that I would say such a thing, snapping that I made it sound as though they were abusing us. They completely ignored the fact that I had made it clear I was joking and that the social worker already knew the bruises had come from the boating. She obviously understood that because my comment was never written down in our case notes. However, they brought that incident up over and over again, using it as evidence that we were liars, as they became increasingly disillusioned with us.

A few months later there was an evening when Pete had had a lot to drink and was becoming quite aggressive towards his wife. I was genuinely worried for her, remembering some of the scenes I had witnessed between Mum and Dad when we were small. Cathy was sitting with me and crying because of the way he was

149

behaving, making all sorts of drunken allegations against her.

'Why don't you sleep in the spare room tonight?' I suggested to her, thinking that would give him a chance to cool down.

Somehow that got turned round and reported to the social workers as me 'wanting her to sleep on the sofa in order to replicate the situation we had experienced at home'. This was despite the fact that she admitted she couldn't remember the incident properly the morning after. She certainly didn't mention to them that she had stripped completely naked in front of me before getting into the bed, an event I found extremely embarrassing, not least because she was so grossly overweight.

'You're trying to make our lives hell,' she accused me, 'just like it was in your house.'

The social workers always seemed to believe everything our foster parents told them about us, and never believed anything we said. It was as if we were banging our heads against a brick wall all the time, trying to explain how we felt and what we needed from the relationship. I've got our case notes now and reading about that time, it is obvious that the adults all thought that the breakdown in our relationship with our foster parents was caused almost wholly by us, not them.

By the winter of 2002–3, they had started actively to resent us for not appreciating them enough. Everything about our past seemed to annoy them from then on. They had strong anti-religious views and when they found out that we had been regular churchgoers all through our childhood they talked in a derogatory manner about it. I didn't feel strongly enough about Christianity to believe I needed to defend it, but I didn't like the suggestion that Mum had done something wrong by involving us in church activities. They seemed to be looking down on us, as if believing in God made us stupid, even though we were still children. They could never resist making snide comments about it whenever the opportunity arose. Everyone, I feel, deserves to have their views respected, especially in a situation where you are trying to build a relationship of mutual trust.

It was beginning to feel as if everyone was judging the way we had lived when Mum was alive. There had been the newspaper articles that made the whole family sound really dysfunctional, and then the curious looks we would get at school, and the way social workers we knew nothing about seemed to be organising our lives from behind the scenes without even discussing it with us, and now we had foster parents pronouncing judgements on our past. I was beginning to feel very defensive of Mum. She had put in so many years of self-sacrifice and hard work for us, for her pupils at school and for Dad, that she didn't deserve to be judged by anyone, especially people who didn't know the whole story in the way we did. The more people said things like that, the more Alex and I would protest about how much fun we had all had together over the years, trying to redress the balance in favour of Mum's memory. The more they disrespected our past, the more determined I became not to enjoy anything they might try to do for us now.

At some point we were told we had been assigned a solicitor, who would liaise with our 'guardian ad liteum' in order to represent our views in the care proceedings. That solicitor realised that no one had thought about sorting out Mum's estate, which only consisted of her share of the house but would still give us a lump of money to help us get established in our adult lives. We kept having meetings with people who we assumed would advise us, but nothing happened once the meetings were over. It seemed almost impossible to get anything done and move forward with our lives.

At the same time, I was struggling with my own private grief. My feelings were all complicated and mixed-up: I felt angry with Dad, of course, and with Helen and Steve, Cathy and Pete; I missed Mum terribly and longed for her with a physical pain that was almost unbearable at times; and I felt determined to protect Alex as best I could. Sometimes I had flashbacks to horrible memories of arguments between Mum and Dad, or other terrifying things that had happened at home, and I'd frequently have horrific nightmares about what

Mum must have gone through during her final minutes of life. I kept all this bottled up and just tried to deal with it on my own. I didn't know what else to do. Who would I have talked to?

Years later, I read in my psychological reports from the time that I was suffering from a raft of disorders, particularly post-traumatic stress and obsessive-compulsive disorder, brought on by what I had gone through over the years of living with Dad and the awful circumstances of Mum's death. All of this must surely have been exacerbated by the lack of understanding and consideration I experienced in Cathy and Pete's home. I was having trouble keeping my head above water, without the added stress of continual arguments under their roof.

Chapter Thirteen

Alex

When our foster parents first told us they would give us twenty pounds a week pocket money each from whatever they were being paid by social services to look after us, it sounded like loads of money compared with what Mum had been able to give us. We soon realised, however, that it wasn't that generous because we were expected to buy all our clothes out of it. We also had to pay any bus fares in and out of town if we wanted to see our friends, which meant the money hardly lasted at all. We could only afford to socialise once a week at the most.

We were never quite sure how Cathy and Pete had made their money in the first place, but they talked a lot about stocks and shares they had bought or sold, and property too. He stayed at home all the time but she had an office job in London, which she would disappear off to on the train every day. I think it was something to do with a housing association. Even though they seemed to have a fair bit of money they were always on the lookout for a bargain, buying knock-off trainers and things like that.

Isobel took her GCSEs in May 2002, just four months after Mum's murder, and managed to get all A's and A stars, apparently putting her amongst the top two or three per cent in the country. Whatever foundations Mum had laid in her when it came to working and not allowing anything to distract her had paid off. She revised like a demon in the final month before the exams to make up for all the distractions we had had over the previous months. When the results came through, she went very quiet and I know that she was missing Mum terribly and feeling desperately sad that she wasn't there, because she would have been so proud.

I was doing okay too; the teachers certainly didn't seem to have any worries or complaints about my work. I liked doing schoolwork because it gave my life some continuity and structure when everything else seemed to be uncertain and up in the air. By keeping our eyes on the goals that Mum had set so firmly for us in the early years we were able to shut out the things that were more difficult to deal with, like emotions, for most of the day. I still seemed to give people the impression that I was messing around a bit in class, so even Isobel was surprised when it came to my turn to sit GCSEs and I did much better than predicted. They'd thought I would only get E's but I managed mostly A's and B's with one C.

It was harder to keep friendships going when we were so far out of town. Isobel had started to lose touch with some of her friends anyway because she had chosen to do sciences at A level and most of them had gone for the arts and drama subjects. If you aren't in the same classes as people you inevitably start to drift apart, particularly if you aren't living in the same area as them. Isobel then lost contact with her other friends simply because she was never available when they wanted to go out together, and our foster parents weren't prepared to drive us around just to socialise. We didn't know anyone who lived in the streets around our foster parents' house because they all went to different schools, so we were pretty much on our own whenever we were at home, sitting around the house, feeling bored. It was a new experience for us. Whatever might have gone on at our family home, we had never had time to become bored.

Every so often Cathy and Pete would do enormously extravagant spur-of-the-moment things, like taking us on holidays to Majorca and to Cuba. They did it because they were used to having four holidays a year themselves and once they had taken on the responsibility of looking after us, they had no option but to take us along. It was kind of them to spend the money, but if they had asked us what we would actually have liked to do, I don't think going on holiday with them would have been high on our list. What we really wanted was more help and support so we could continue to live our normal lives in England, seeing our friends and doing all the things we had always done. Family holidays can be stressful even when you go with your own parents, never mind a couple you hardly know and don't particularly like.

I think Cathy felt much the same because once we were on holiday she would almost immediately become irritated that Isobel and I were hanging around them too much, being a bit nervous to go off on our own in a foreign country. We had never been abroad with Mum so I think it is understandable that we were wary.

'Why don't you go off and do something?' she would protest, wanting some holiday time to herself. Ironically, it was the opposite of what she had been saying at home when she was trying to persuade us to spend more time with them.

It was a bit of a Catch 22 situation for her because I dare say the money they earned for having us was what made a lot of their lifestyle possible, but then having two teenagers lurking around was spoiling that lifestyle once she had it. Isobel and I did do some things on our own, like going on a scuba-diving course together, but there were a lot of hours in the day when we were just relaxing around the hotels, like all the other families there.

I can imagine we came across as being a bit ungrateful and resentful at times like that, not able to get into the holiday spirit in the way they might have hoped we

no one listened

would. There was a canal boat holiday too, which forced us all into very close proximity. It took us three and a half days to cover a distance that would have taken us an hour to drive. We had real trouble seeing the point of the exercise. Cathy and Pete would always end up being angry with us for obviously not enjoying ourselves as much as they had hoped we would. I guess we must have been a disappointment to them, but the very fact that they thought we would enjoy it showed they knew as little about us as we did about them.

It was claustrophobic being in the house when Isobel and I had such different expectations of what we wanted from the relationship to Cathy and Pete. We were typical teenagers in many ways and tensions that in an ordinary family would have been balanced with an underlying love, started to flare up through the polite façade we were all trying hard to maintain. There was one occasion when Cathy got so annoyed with Isobel after she had had a few drinks that she chased her upstairs with a wineglass still in her hand. Thinking she was going to get the glass lobbed at her, Isobel ran upstairs and took refuge in her room, shaking uncontrollably, suddenly having a flashback to all the angry, unpredictable altercations with Dad.

Cathy burst into the room and was so angry she kept hitting Isobel on the arm with the base of the empty glass. Isobel didn't respond, just staying stock still, which seemed to annoy Cathy even more, making her hit even harder until she eventually got bored and went back downstairs. The next morning when Isobel woke up she found she had massive bruising stretching from her elbow to her shoulder. It was so bad her teacher noticed it in school and took her to one side to ask how it had happened.

'I just walked into a door,' Isobel said, not wanting to start a whole load more trouble. There was a social worker due at the house a few days later and Cathy and Pete told Isobel to wear a long-sleeved jumper for the visit so the bruises wouldn't be visible.

From then on we were both walking on eggshells all the time, just as we used to around Dad, aware that we might spark off their anger and resentment at any moment.

Early in 2003, Isobel realised that the solicitor we had hired to sort out Mum's estate didn't seem to be achieving anything. She was sixteen by then, almost seventeen, and she took the decision to sack him and handle everything herself. When she rang to tell him that she didn't want him working on our case any more he actually thanked her, saying that it was so complicated he had felt overwhelmed by everything that needed to be done. I remember wondering how Isobel was going to manage on her own if a qualified solicitor felt overwhelmed but she was getting quite good at that sort of thing. She then had a battle with that first solicitor because he was trying to charge us for his time when he hadn't actually done anything. She stood up for herself and managed to resolve the situation, which I thought was pretty impressive.

She found us a new solicitor in Evesham but it would still be several years before the whole thing was sorted out because there were all sorts of complications. For example, we found out that Mum's direct debits were still leaving her bank account six months after she died and her bank wanted us to repay them. Isobel seemed to spend her whole life chasing things like Mum's birth certificate, marriage certificate and death certificate. The social services wanted to be my financial guardian and trustee since Isobel was still under 18 but we didn't trust them to make the best decisions. There was so much paperwork to wade through and so many phone calls to make, so much waiting for people to come back to us and then chasing them up that it sometimes seemed as though we would never reach the end of the maze, that we would be sorting out the mess Dad made the day Mum died for the rest of our lives. I don't know what I would have done if I hadn't had Isobel to bear the brunt of it.

Chapter Fourteen

Isobel

The antipathy between us and our foster parents was growing all the time and it was becoming increasingly difficult to maintain the charade that we liked one another. I could tell how much I annoyed them, particularly Cathy. If we ever sat next to each other on the sofa, watching telly, she would hold my arm and pinch me or dig her nails in painfully. It was as if she couldn't resist the urge to inflict pain and show me how she felt about me and how frustrated I made her feel, even if we weren't actually arguing about anything at the time. Only later, when I was given our social services files of the time, did I read that she was saying it was me doing that to her rather than the other way round. That made me absolutely furious!

It was when I protested one evening that she was hurting me that she got angry and chased me up the stairs and hit me with her wineglass. It was as if she believed I was making the whole thing up just to make her look bad. I never told any of the social workers about the way our relationship was breaking down, mainly because I had no idea how to get in contact with them without asking our foster parents for the telephone number, a request that had never gone down well in the past. For several months Alex and I didn't even have a social worker assigned to us, and on the rare occasion when someone did turn up they would always talk to us in front of Cathy and Pete, so there was no chance for us to say what was truly on our minds without risking offending them even more.

Most of the time I kept quiet and tried not to argue, bottling up all my frustrations and resentments, hoping that I could keep things peaceful that way. But by just sitting there and saying nothing I probably appeared sullen and rude, and if I got up and left the room in order to remove myself from the temptation to respond, it would look as if I was storming off in a tantrum. I couldn't find a way of handling the day-to-day situation that didn't give the wrong impression and make things worse between us.

It was so frustrating to be dependent on people we didn't really like and who didn't really like us. We were being treated as if we were still small children even though I was now almost seventeen, virtually an adult. Nobody would talk openly and honestly to us about what was going on, and it was only as the date of Dad's trial drew near that we discovered all the adults around us knew something devastating about us that we didn't know and could never have imagined.

Social services and the police had all known about this particular bombshell since looking at Mum's medical reports. Jillian and Helen had also told the police in their interviews. Even our foster parents had known and never said a word, which was very out of character. We later found out that the police had hoped the doctors would tell us the terrible truth, but the doctors had refused and batted the responsibility straight back to them. They then passed the task on to a psychologist who worked at The Priory in London, the place where all the celebrities go to deal with their addiction problems. We had no idea this was all going on and so in January 2003 when we were told we were going to London to see a psychologist we assumed it was just for another routine interview to gather evidence for the care proceedings.

We had only met this man twice before, when social services first needed a psychological report on us for the care courts, so it is hard to imagine why everyone thought he was the best person to break such a distressing bit of news to us. We were told we were going to see him again, but no one said why and we didn't bother to ask. We had grown used to going where we were told without understanding any of the logic behind what was happening. Our foster parents drove us to London in their car and two social workers followed independently. We didn't bother to ask any questions; it never did any good and we didn't know what to ask anyway.

'We need to tell you this now,' the psychologist said when we finally arrived at his office in The Priory, 'because otherwise you will find out in the courtroom. Your mother had Huntington's disease.'

The news meant nothing to us. Neither of us had ever heard of Huntington's, but he went on to explain what it would have meant to Mum and what it might mean to us. The disease, he said, is caused by the degeneration of nerve-cell clusters in the brain. As it takes a hold the affected person starts to make rapid, jerky, involuntary movements and they gradually descend into dementia. Most people don't start to see any symptoms until they are about thirty-five years old. The disease is hereditary and there is always a fifty-fifty chance that any child of a sufferer will also have it. That meant the chances were that either Alex or I would have inherited it, if not both of us. There was a test for it, the psychologist explained, but we weren't allowed by law to take that test until we were eighteen. So we now knew there was a fifty-fifty chance we had a degenerative disease but I wasn't allowed to find out for sure until my eighteenth birthday in a year and a quarter's time, and Alex would have to live with the uncertainty for another two years after that.

Huntington's only happens to between five and eight people in every hundred thousand. Most of those diagnosed only live for between fifteen and thirty years after the onset of the symptoms. There is no known cure. The symptoms usually start with the sufferer making random grimaces and twitches and becoming clumsy. As the dementia sets in they become irritable and difficult, have trouble making decisions, lose their memory and are overcome with feelings of apathy. Images of Mum in the last year or two of her life kept flashing in front of my eyes as I listened to the psychologist's description. Had she had any symptoms of the disease? Or was her short fuse just due to exhaustion and stress?

Ten minutes after we had walked into his office, having informed us of all these stark facts, the psychologist said goodbye. We returned to the cars to drive back out of London as we tried to take in everything we had been told. Thinking back, I guessed that this must have been what had killed our grandmother early, not cancer, and I also realised that Mum must have known she had it. When she became so depressed and tried to kill herself she must already have known that she would soon be an invalid and would probably die prematurely anyway. She must have been afraid she was going to be a burden to us and an increasing source of annoyance to Dad. So by taking her life she wouldn't have been acting as selfishly as we had thought; she might actually have been thinking of what was best for Alex and me all along. Since she hadn't told us about her breast cancer until the day of the operation, it was no surprise that she had kept the Huntington's a secret as well.

Staring at the backs of our foster parents' heads in the car home it was hard to imagine that they had known about the Huntington's for so many months when we hadn't a clue about it. I didn't hold back on telling them how annoyed I was with them. In some ways I had started to feel I could trust them over the previous few months, even if I didn't particularly like them, and now I found they had been keeping a secret like this, I felt massively betrayed and told them so.

'The police and the social workers told us we mustn't tell you,' they explained. 'They said there was no point because you couldn't take the test yet anyway.'

'So why have they changed their minds now?'

'Because it's all going to come out in court.'

In a strange way the news didn't make us feel particularly frightened – just angry. After everything that had happened to us over the previous year it just felt like one more thing we had to contend with, something else we had no power over. In a way I thought that perhaps after so much had happened to us it would be too much of a coincidence for one or both of us to have a life-threatening disease as well. Surely fate couldn't be that unkind to us after we'd lost our mother in such a traumatic way?

So, as usual, I put it to the back of my mind, deciding I would deal with the problem once I was old enough to take the test.

The date of Dad's trial kept being put off as the police tried to build their case against him and his defence lawyers tried to build up medical evidence about him and about Mum to rationalise and excuse what he had done. To us it seemed like one thing after another holding them up. It felt as though no one in the whole adult world was in any hurry to find out exactly what had happened in our house that day and to punish Dad for what he had done. Until the trial happened the whole house belonged to Dad because as her husband he would automatically inherit Mum's half, which meant we owned little more than the clothes we stood up in.

During those thirteen months of waiting in his comfortable remand prison, Dad had had time to think up a sort of defence with his lawyers, but none of it made much sense to anyone else who listened to it. At moments he seemed to be pleading with the authorities to jail him because that would take away all the worries that he had found so difficult to cope with while surviving in the outside world. We could believe that he was being sincere when he asked to be sent down. Jail would suit his personality; he was never a man who wanted to talk to people if he didn't have to. He wouldn't have started any aggro with other prisoners unless someone else picked on him first, and they would soon learn to give him a wide berth. Even when he was living with us he had always behaved as though he was already in a prison, spending most of his days in his 'cell', passing us by on the landing and not even acknowledging us, always seeking out his own space away from us.

'"Give me twenty years" – pleads wife killer,' was the way the headline writers portrayed his plea.

The authorities weren't keen on us attending the court, saying that we shouldn't really miss so much school, but we fought hard to be allowed in. We were both in a good position with our schoolwork and exams and it wasn't going to affect us too much if we missed a few days. We thought that to be reading about the case in the papers and having to go into school knowing that everyone else was seeing and hearing what was said would be much harder than actually hearing it for ourselves. Thank God we did go because there was lots of bad stuff about Mum said at the beginning and we wouldn't have wanted to go back to school until the whole story had been told, and we had got our version across.

We were fed up with being left on the outside of things that were vitally important to us while everyone else got to talk about us as if we had no minds of our own. It was our family and our lives they were all going to be discussing; why shouldn't we be there to listen and put our points of view? When it was decided we could give evidence as witnesses, it seemed even more ridiculous that we should do that and not be allowed to stay and hear what everyone else was saying about us and about our Mum. Eventually they gave in and we were given permission to attend the whole trial.

Our barrister was a lovely woman and was very worried about calling us as witnesses in case the experience proved to be too traumatic for us. Initially the police agreed with her and didn't want us to have to go through the ordeal either, maybe because they remembered how immature we had been when they first interviewed us a year before. In the end it was Dad's barrister who decided we needed to be called. I think he had heard our interview tapes with the police and underestimated how much we had grown up since then, and how good we had become at defending ourselves when talking to adults. The police interview had happened the day after the killing, when we still didn't really understand what was going on. We could be heard laughing and joking on the tapes, which gave completely the wrong impression of how we were going to be presenting our case this time. It had only been in the ensuing weeks and months that even a portion of the truth about what had happened to our Mum began to sink in. In fact we still didn't know the whole story and would learn a shocking amount by listening to the other witnesses in the following days.

I'm the first to admit that I was not the most mature of fifteen-year-olds. As long as Mum was alive I had been able to remain pretty immature because she did everything for us and I never had to take responsibility for anything. Alex was still just a kid. The year since she died had been a steep and painful learning curve for both of us and neither of us were the same children we had been that day.

Dad's barrister must have thought he would be able to make us look like difficult, nightmare children and bully us into crumbling and admitting that our Dad was a wonderful person really and that Mum had driven him to do what he did. But we were pretty sure that no reasonable jury was going to believe that and we were both confident that we could stand up to any amount of questioning.

Our barrister kindly arranged for us to be taken to visit the court a couple of days before the trial started in order to see the layout of the courtroom and meet some of the people who would be there on the day, just to get us used to the environment. I think the police had recommended that we do this as well. Not many people had shown us that much consideration over the previous year.

When the trial opened on 3rd February 2003, we were both very nervous. Our foster parents came along with us and they seemed to enjoy it rather like they might an extended West End show, making jokes and comments about things that had been said in the courtroom all the way home in the car. Two of Mum's cousins made the odd day visit to the court too but they chatted to our foster parents more than to us. The family liaison officer sat through it with us and our social worker came on the days when we were giving our evidence, so they could go off and write another report about us that we wouldn't get to see for several years.

This was going to be the first glimpse we had had of our father for over a year, since he was led from the house to the police car. Even though we were confident we could stand up to questioning from his barrister, we were still as frightened of Dad as we had always been. A fear that has been with you for so many years, day in and day out, doesn't vanish overnight, however much you might be able to rationalise it away in your mind.

When he was brought into the courtroom he looked different to how I remembered him. If anything he looked more frightening than he had when he was shuffling in and out of his bedroom, or sitting in the kitchen glowering at us. He seemed to have bulked up and with his shaved head and angry scowl he looked like a proper skinhead thug. I suppose I was seeing him for the first time as the rest of the world saw him and I was able to understand why all the neighbours had been so wary of him for all those years.

After a load of preliminaries, which seemed to last forever, they started putting their case and I was shocked by how Dad's barrister laid into Mum's memory, making out that it was all her fault that Dad had run amok and killed her. It had never occurred to me that a murder victim could be made to sound as though they had brought it on themselves, as if she had somehow provoked him into killing her, as if he was some bad-tempered old dog that kids should be careful not to tease.

Dad refused to take the witness stand throughout the trial, so instead the police played the tapes of his initial interrogation, so the jury could hear everything he had to say at the time. The problem with that for our side was that our barrister never got a chance to cross-examine him about any of the claims and statements he made. If she had been able to do that she could very quickly have discredited virtually everything he had to say. As it was, his taped words hung in the air unchallenged and we realised we were going to have to work hard to put our side of the story.

Asked by the police interviewers to explain what had driven him to kill her, Dad told them that it was all because of Mum and us and the way we behaved towards him. He told them how much he hated us and how miserable we made his life. He said that the onset of Huntington's had made Mum irritable and forgetful and difficult to live with. This was rubbish; when Mum's

172

doctor came to the stand, he explained that she had only just started developing symptoms such as slight memory loss and twitching. Listening to Dad talking I understood why the social services had been forced to find a way to tell us about the disease; otherwise it would have come as even more of a shock to hear it talked about for the first time by strangers in a courtroom.

Mum, according to him, was always neglecting her duties as a housewife and there was always out-of-date food in the house. When the police looked into that accusation the only out-of-date food they could find were some old packets of crisps I'd chucked up on top of the fridge when Mum gave them to me because I didn't like crisps. Dad also claimed the house was dirty and Mum never cleaned it, which wasn't true – and anyway he was the one who was supposed to be staying at home to look after us while Mum was out at work earning the money to support us all. The house may have been a bit shabby, because Mum chose to spend her time and money on us while he chose to spend it on drink and locking himself in his room, but it was no dirtier or untidier than any other busy family home.

He claimed that he was anxious because he had no money, and that had been another factor driving him to act desperately. But we knew the lack of money was not really at the root of anything because Mum always gave him whatever he asked for, and always had. It may be that he had kept back a few savings from when he had worked for a short time delivering parcels, a job he claimed he took to make himself feel more independent, and that that money had finally run out. But if that was the problem he could easily have found himself another job that would have earned him as much since he had no other calls on his time. There was never anything stopping him from working apart from his own hatred of the outside world and everyone in it.

Another of his claims was that he didn't like me having friends in the house, particularly boys. He tried to give the impression that I was sleeping around, but as I was always a tomboy nearly all my friends were boys anyway, and they hardly ever came to the house because I was afraid of aggravating Dad. They all thought he was weird and preferred to steer clear. I'd only ever invited people back twice when I was about thirteen. Both times I did it because I thought Dad was out and we wanted to work together on school projects. When he came downstairs unexpectedly and found strangers invading space that he saw as exclusively his, he exploded and threw them out of the house, which I found pretty hard to explain to them the next day. In court Dad insisted it was all to do with sex, which anyone who knew me at that age would have known was ridiculous. All I thought about was school work and sport and other after-school activities.

Although his barrister was calling us to give evidence in order to discredit us, from our barrister's point of view we were potentially the most effective character witnesses that she could have hoped for. Our evidence seemed to be by far the strongest of all the witnesses'. Hardly anyone else knew anything about Dad since he had spent most of the previous few years in his bedroom. They might have heard the shouting late at night, or heard stories of some of the more outrageous things he got up to, but none of them had had to live under the same roof as him for years on end, witnessing every piece of weirdness and unpleasantness. His lawyer must have been desperate to discredit us in any way he could because without us no one would have any real idea of what went on behind the closed doors of our home.

Since nothing much that had happened in our life in the previous year had made any logical sense to us, it was always at the back of our minds that Dad might possibly be found not guilty for some technical legal reason, and would then be free to walk out of the court at the end of the trial. Because we were terrified of what he might do to us if that happened, we and the social services had always gone to great lengths to keep our new location secret. The judge, however, called our foster mother to the stand and insisted that she gave her full name and address for the whole courtroom, including Dad, to hear. It suddenly seemed even more imperative that he was convicted and didn't get to walk the streets again for a long time.

When it was time for me to give my evidence, I was led out of the court to another small room where I gave evidence into a video camera.

'Did you get in trouble once at school?' his barrister asked me.

I assumed he was referring to the shoplifting incident. 'Maybe,' I admitted. 'Doesn't everyone get into trouble at school sometimes?'

It was as if neither Dad nor his barrister had the slightest idea what normal family life was like or how normal children could be expected to behave. We were two of the hardest-working, highest-achieving kids in our school, despite the fact that Alex occasionally got into trouble for being a bit bolshie. If we had done anything wrong at home, it would have been the kind of things that a normal father would have sorted out with a few strong words. In fact, Dad had always egged Alex on to misbehave as much as possible because he knew it annoyed Mum and made him feel less like the odd one out in the family.

The barrister had a trick of leaving long pauses at the end of each of my answers in the hope that I would stumble on and say something that would help his case. But each time he did it I jumped in with another example of the horrible things Dad did around the house. After a bit he got the point and stopped doing the pausing.

I gave evidence for most of the first day of the trial, then they said that Alex and I had to stay in separate places that night so we couldn't compare notes, so he was sent to a hotel. Once Alex had answered all his questions, it was time for the police tapes of Dad's interrogation to be played to the court.

All through his recorded statement Dad seemed to be obsessed with sex, even though it was a subject that had never come up when we were together as a family. He insisted that I was promiscuous; that Mum had slept with one of her pupils; and that Alex was being interfered with by a neighbour when he was about seven years old. I actually had to ask what the word 'promiscuous' meant, and neither of us had any memory of there ever being a man living next door, let alone a paedophile. Alex had never been abused by anyone; he didn't even know such things happened. When the lawyer sprang those sorts of questions on me for the first time I actually laughed, partly from shock and partly because I thought he must be joking. What was so surprising was that Dad's barrister hadn't even bothered to check if there was a man living next door to us at any point, nor had he approached the school to ask about the other children who were supposed to have been coming to the house for sex with me. If he had, he would have been told that we were all part of the same study group and that we sometimes met to discuss our projects. As it was he made his accusations in front of the whole courtroom and was left looking foolish.

Dad sat completely still in the dock, his face immobile throughout the trial, showing no glimmer of emotion. It almost looked as if he had been sedated and couldn't hear what was going on around him. The stillness added to the eerie feeling of danger and evil that seemed to envelop him. Maybe he was doing it on purpose to intimidate the witnesses. At one point in the proceedings I was staring at him, trying to work out what might be going through his mind behind those dead eyes, trying to see if there was any reaction to anything that was being said about him, when he suddenly leant forward and muttered something to his barrister. The barrister glanced across at me and went up to whisper something to the judge.

The judge listened to whatever it was he had to say and then he too looked across at me. 'If you continue to look at the accused in that manner, young lady,' he warned, 'I am going to have to refuse you entry to the courtroom.'

I've got no idea how I was looking at him, but maybe my hatred showed on my face. It seemed strange to me that Dad had the right to demand that I didn't look at him when he was sitting at the centre of the proceedings, directly in everyone's line of vision. Did he really feel that threatened by me? Was he just trying to demonstrate to the judge and jury what an intimidating child I was, to show how intolerable it must have been to have to live with me? Or was he trying to remind me that he still had some control over me? It seemed particularly unfair since both Alex and I were nervous that as more and more was said against him he might grow angry, lose his self-control and jump up and attack us. He was seated only a couple of metres away from us. It was obvious that the things that were being said were going to be winding him up and he had made it very clear how much he hated us. We already knew he was capable of making a frenzied attack on someone who annoyed him and I had worked out that the woman who was supposed to be guarding us was sitting too far away to be able to get to us in time if Dad did decide to make a lunge. Since he was trying to get away with a plea of 'diminished responsibil- ity' he wouldn't lose much by attacking us in full view of a courtroom; in fact, he might even be confirming in the eyes of the judge and jury that he was insane and should be sectioned rather than sentenced. All these thoughts were constantly coursing around in my brain as I sat listening to the voices of the lawyers and officials dron- ing on, trying not to look at him.

As another part of his explanation to the police about why he had gone berserk with a chisel, Dad started talk- ing about how he had been abused as a child, as if that was a reason for stabbing his wife to death. The court didn't seem to show any interest in this information. I suppose it is likely that he had a difficult childhood, as one of twelve children, but he had never talked to us about it before.

All through the previous year he had been attempting to prove that he was mentally disturbed and various psychologists had spent time with him trying to ascertain if that was the case. None of them, however, could come up with anything beyond 'a mild personality disorder'. They did say he had a touch of obsessive-compulsive disorder, or OCD, which might have explained why he found it difficult to cope with us when we interrupted his routines, but that hardly gave him a reason for murdering someone. He claimed that it was the OCD that caused him to become agitated when the house was messy and things were not in their right places. Since he spent virtually all his time in his bedroom and was seldom in any other room in the house, it is hard to see how that could have been a major problem.

I understand quite a bit about OCD because I had been diagnosed with it myself. I think it is quite common amongst people who feel they don't have control in their own lives and so they become obsessive about the little things they can control. My condition became worse at Cathy and Pete's when my habits and anxieties started to become more complex. I would have to go through an increasing number of routines every time I left the house or before I could go to bed, checking windows and doors over and over again, insisting on turning off electrical appliances whenever they weren't in use, wanting to feel completely secure and free of anxiety before I could hope to relax and sleep. They used to shout at me angrily when they went to use the kettle and found that I had turned it off at the mains since they last used it. It actually used to annoy me as much as it annoyed them, but I couldn't stop myself. Alex was a little bit the same, although he wasn't so obsessive about routines as I was. His main symptom was lining things up neatly in rows. Maybe we inherited it from Dad. I certainly wouldn't think of using it as an excuse for murder, though.

At one point in his police interrogation Dad claimed that neither of us were really his children, as if Mum was sleeping around all through their marriage, which was completely laughable. It did make us wonder, however, if things like that had happened in his family, and that was why he imagined, or claimed to imagine, that we were living a similar sort of life? Maybe he was abused as a child and maybe there were women in his family who had children that didn't belong to their husbands. I doubt we'll ever know now.

It was hard to sit there and listen as Dad came out with one lie after another and not say anything. My instincts were to shout out that it was all untrue but I knew that would just reflect badly on me. At one point he claimed that he never even knew Mum had cancer. I suppose he wanted to show that she cared for him so little she hadn't even told him something as important as that. But I knew he had picked her up from the hospital after her operation, so he was blatantly lying. I remembered the incident clearly because it was so out of character for him to do anything for any of us. Helen just got a phone call telling her not to worry about picking Mum up because Dad had already done it.

All I could do when I heard these lies on the tapes was jot down notes and pass them to our barrister, because we had said our bit by then and we weren't going to get another chance. Because Dad never took the stand himself she never had the chance to cross-examine him about any of the claims he made in his police interview or that his barrister was making on his behalf.

As we listened to all the barrister's arguments, Alex and I were both becoming truly frightened that he would be let off for some technical reason and would be back out on the street as soon as the case was finished. We had been left in no doubt about the depth of his hatred for us and we were sure he would come looking for us as soon as he could. At least if he was imprisoned for a good few years he would have time to cool off and we would have had time to move away from the area and establish lives for ourselves. Surely the judge would be able to see how dangerous he was? Our faith in the authorities had been shaken so badly by this time that we weren't convinced they would be able to protect us if Dad was released. It was a nerve-racking two weeks, to say the least.

Chapter Fifteen

Alex

Although we were allowed to sit in the court during the trial listening to everyone else, we had to sit in another room and talk to a video camera when giving our evidence, which meant that we couldn't see the reactions of anyone else in the courtroom to our answers. The only person we could see was the lawyer who was actually questioning us from the television screen in front of us. I didn't like the idea that Dad would be thinking he could control us and frighten us into giving our evidence from another room. Even though it was true that we were frightened of him, I would have liked to show him I wasn't scared by giving evidence while sitting just a few feet away from him. I would like to have seen his reactions to the things I had to say – although he probably wouldn't have reacted at all because he hardly did to anything else that was said about him.

Later we were told by people who had been in the courtroom while we were being cross-examined that the jury and all the other people listening had seemed to be completely on our side while we were giving evidence. They said that we made them laugh and that our down-to-earth descriptions of our family life made Dad's accusations seem all the more wild and fantastical.

Isobel gave her evidence first and was on the stand – or in front of the camera – for a whole day. I wasn't allowed to listen, either in the court or in the room with her, in case her answers influenced what I said when it came to my turn to be cross-examined the following day. That night we had to be kept separate, with me in a hotel room, in case Isobel tried to brief me on what she had said and what traps I should be wary of falling into. Dad's barrister wanted to be able to spring the allegations he had made against me to my face without me having been forewarned by Isobel. I knew that the biggest danger was that I would become angry about the things Dad's barrister was saying, which would make me look like an unreliable witness, so I was determined to stay calm and get it right. There was too much depending on it.

The following day, while I was in the other room talking to the camera, there was a party of school kids shown into the courtroom, just to have a look around. Isobel got really irritated because they kept giggling and messing about and in the end she shouted at them to be quiet, which got her a telling off from the judge. It was probably pretty boring to them, but to Isobel it seemed as though they were being disrespectful about Mum's murder and our bereavement. In the end the judge had to ask the kids to leave the courtroom because of their behaviour and I dare say it was a relief for them to get out.

When you are so emotionally involved in a case it is incredibly frustrating to see other people treating it casually. An event that had changed our entire lives and devastated our family was just a professional engagement for most of the people in the room, and a gruesome sort of entertainment for the rest. At one point Isobel spotted a member of the jury falling asleep during the medical reports, but she managed to keep quiet about that. To be fair the medical stuff did go on for about a day and a half and was pretty boring, but still it seemed that staying awake should have been the minimum requirement for a jury member in a murder case. Isobel managed to hold her tongue since no one else in the court appeared to be worried about it.

Everything the barrister threw at me over the video link was easily answered. Most of Dad's accusations were patently ludicrous and figments of a delusional imagination, and just by giving a straight account of how things had been at home I was able to make that point. In fact I did so well they asked if Isobel had coached me in what to say the previous night. She wouldn't have needed to coach me in anything even if she'd been allowed to. It was completely obvious what answers to give; all I had to remember was not lose my temper. People told us that we just had to tell the truth and justice would automatically be done. We wanted to believe that was true, but we still weren't completely confident that some technicality wouldn't arise that would give Dad a loophole to escape through.

The only time his defence team came close to making us look delinquent during those video-links was when they asked about Isobel's reprimand for shoplifting. Dad never said anything about it at the time but he must have been storing it up to use against her and now he hoped that by branding her as a thief and a liar in court he could discredit everything she said about him. It was the first and last time she had ever done anything like it, and half her class at school had been caught shoplifting at least once, so it wasn't a very big deal. Isobel had never made any attempt to deny it and bringing the matter up still didn't convince anyone in the courtroom that either of us had ever given Dad any excuse to do what he had done.

Another of his claims was that he was worried he was going to run out of money, but since Mum was his main source of income that didn't make sense either. Why would he kill the person who was supplying him with food and drink and a roof over his head? Then there was all the nonsense about Mum being terrible at looking after the house. The defending lawyer thought he had tricked Isobel by asking if there was any out-of-date food in the house and then springing the evidence of the crisps that the police had found when she denied all knowledge of it. Apparently the jury actually laughed out loud when she explained about chucking the packets up there herself just because she didn't like crisps. Although we couldn't judge, I imagine all our answers came across as normal and believable, because we had no reason to lie about anything, while Dad's arguments were sounding less and less believable as he piled on new complaints.

Even if everything he had said was true and we had been the terrible children he claimed we were, and Mum had been the worst housewife in the world, it hardly explained why he would have felt the need to stab her more than fifty times. The whole trial was like something from *Alice in Wonderland*.

They called Helen to the witness stand and it emerged that she had always referred to him as 'Mad Bert', a fact that his lawyers jumped on to help prove that Dad was suffering from diminished responsibility, that he was indeed 'mad' rather than just plain 'bad'. There had been endless psychiatric assessments done of him in attempts to ascertain the truth, but all the doctors agreed that he was quite sane enough to know what he was doing that day. The defence team wanted to suggest that Dad's state of mind and his behaviour had all had something to do with the stroke he suffered when I was in the house on my own with him. They wanted to show that he had been perfectly fine until that moment. The police, on the other hand, had found plenty of witnesses from the neighbourhood who were willing to talk to them at length about the things Dad had been getting up to from the first day he moved in, many years before he suffered his stroke. Isobel and I were too young to be able to give any reliable evidence about what he was like before that day, although neither of us had any memories of him ever being any different.

Until the trial no one had ever really talked to us about what had happened on the day of the murder. We learned almost everything that had been excluded from the newspaper reports for the first time in court – like the fact that an elderly couple living in a nearby bungalow had heard screams but thought they were coming from children playing out in the street and so did nothing about them. Details like that would bring the scene horribly to life for us, allowing our imaginations free rein to fill in the rest.

The more facts that were laid out in front of us, the more questions came into our minds. Although we were still puzzled as to why Mum hadn't mentioned that she would be coming home early for her hospital appointment on the day she died, we were willing to accept that she might just have forgotten about it in the rush of being late for work that morning, or that the appointment was changed during the course of that day. But if she did go to the appointment, which the hospital had confirmed she did, how come she was in her comfortable 'home clothes' when her body was found? Even though she had grown more careless about her appearance in her final months, she still had certain standards and whenever she went to a hospital appointment she would always wear her work clothes, which were smarter.

Someone came forward to say they had spotted her driving her car down the road at 3.15 pm, not long before Dad made the calls to the police claiming he had killed her. It seems unlikely she could have changed in those few minutes so she must have done it before. She had left the hospital appointment at 2.10 pm, but it wouldn't have taken her an hour to get home, so we can only assume that at some point she had come home and changed into her casual clothes and had then gone out again in the car for some reason. Isobel and I went over it a thousand times from every angle whenever we were alone together, but whatever way we looked at it there seemed to be forty-five minutes missing from the scenario that the police built up of her final movements. When the forensic experts went into the house to try to work out exactly what had happened, there was a newspaper laid out beside the rocking chair in the dining room. Knowing her habits as we did, that suggested to us that Mum had been sitting in there with the dog to keep him from barking and disturbing Dad.

One of the most distressing things of all was an outline picture produced for the jury that showed the site of all Mum's wounds. Dots marked the spots on her shoulders, collarbone, breastbone and chest where the chisel had punctured, as well as all the wounds on her hands and forearms where she had obviously been trying to defend herself. It gave a graphic depiction of her final, desperate struggle for life that I found horribly upsetting. Every time I tried to imagine what Mum must have gone through in the last moments of her life, I felt sick to the stomach and filled with hatred for Dad.

In court the police played the tapes of the phone calls Dad made to them, in which he told them openly that he had killed his wife and that they needed to get there as quickly as possible because we were on our way home from school. It transpired from their investigations that he had gone upstairs after killing her, changed out of his bloodstained clothes and packed himself a going-away bag, presumably expecting the police to be knocking at the door by the time he came back downstairs. It was almost as if the whole point of killing Mum was to get himself put into a cell somewhere, away from all responsibility and free from all decisions. If that was the case, it was difficult to see how the court was going to be able to punish him for what he had done without giving him exactly the outcome that he was after. Both Isobel and I believe that jail must suit him right down to the ground. It's not a punishment at all for someone like him, who had been living voluntarily in a locked room for many years beforehand.

Chapter Sixteen

Isobel

Dad's lawyers had found one character witness for the defence and they obviously believed they had a good chance of redeeming their client's character through this witness's testimony because of a statement he had given to them when they went to interview him. He was an Italian man whom Dad had worked with briefly at a parcel delivery firm the year before. He was being asked to vouch for Dad being a good worker and a good man. The statement he had made gave them confidence that he would be willing to say these things when questioned. They needed something to counteract all the people who had come forward to say Dad was a terrible husband, father and neighbour.

When this witness climbed onto the stand, however, he said the exact opposite to whatever was in the written version of his statement. Instead of saying Dad 'could' have done something, he was saying Dad 'could not' have done it.

'You do realise that lying in court under oath is a criminal offence for which you could be imprisoned?' the barrister reminded him impatiently, obviously furious that the one straw he had been clinging to looked as though it was being snatched away.

But the Italian stood his ground and swore that he would never have said the words that were in the written statement because he absolutely believed the opposite to be true.

'There has been an error here,' he protested, 'I definitely didn't say that. There is no way I would be standing here saying things in support of this man.'

The barrister kept on at him for nearly an hour but the witness refused to change his story even under the threat of being locked up for perjury. With no other witnesses to turn to, Dad's barrister demanded that the original tape of the interview with the Italian be produced in court and compared to the written statement he was working from. The court was adjourned so they could look into it and they discovered, after hours of time had been wasted, that whoever had transcribed the statement into writing had missed out the word 'not', which was clearly audible on the tape, thereby completely changing the sense of what the man was saying. The witness they had hoped would say positive things about Dad had actually ended up saying negative things. The prosecution team would never have called him as a witness so it was an unexpected bonus for them. It seemed that no one who had ever met Dad had a good word to say for him, not even his own character witness. We were very grateful to the Italian for standing his ground because I doubt if anyone would have gone to check the original tapes if he had caved in to the pressure and agreed that the mistake was his.

A lot of the witnesses were obviously nervous when they had to stand up and speak under his expressionless stare. Jillian was actually shaking and her voice trembling while she talked, but she didn't let it deter her. A lot of the stories the witnesses from our street told about him were the first we knew of the things he had done, like disrupting people's gardens and driving around with a loud hailer on the roof of his van, shouting abuse. Although the things that we had to say must have been an eye-opener for everyone else listening in the courtroom, we had also learned a lot about our own family history by seeing the goings on in our house through the eyes of others. They'd all heard the arguments and the shouting and seen incidents of one sort or another over the years. Mum's doctor was called and all the reports about her Huntington's were read out at length, so it was just as well we'd been warned about this beforehand.

In marked contrast to everything that was being said about Dad, there was only one witness who had anything bad to say about us. She was a neighbour who claimed that I had bullied her daughter, an event I had no memory of whatsoever. As far as I was concerned the girl and I had always been good friends until we had an argument about something and had stopped talking. Even if she had perceived it as bullying, which I couldn't imagine was possible, there didn't seem to be any reason to bring it up in front of the court that was looking into the murder of my mother. I was so hurt and angry, particularly because it had been said at the end of the trial when I couldn't defend myself, that I followed the woman out of the courtroom and started haranguing her in the corridor outside, which got me told off again.

At the end of the two-week trial there were the closing speeches. By the time Dad's barrister was making his there was very little he could say because Dad had made him look a fool with all his fantasies and lies. But he still managed to make his speech last for a day and a half.

No one was suggesting that Dad hadn't killed Mum; it just seemed to come down to whether or not he was sane when he did it and whether Mum had provoked him in some way. When the speeches were finally all over the jury only went out to deliberate for a couple of hours before they returned. The foreman announced that they were unanimous in their verdict of 'guilty'.

Our barrister warned us that when the judge passed his sentence we must be careful not to react, however strongly we might feel about his decision.

'I always find it hard not to say anything,' she admitted, 'but we have to control our emotions out of respect for the judge.'

Despite our barrister's warning we weren't able to stop ourselves from rising to our feet as we turned to hear what the judge had to say. He solemnly announced that the mandatory sentence for murder was life, and he would be recommending that Dad should serve between twenty and twenty-five years, but he didn't actually set the tariff there and then. As we came out our barrister explained to us what was happening.

'At the moment sentences are being set by the Home Office and there is a backlog of cases waiting to be decided,' she said. 'We may not hear the final sentence for some time.'

The police had told us that they thought he would get at least fifteen years as he had shown no remorse for his actions at any stage, unashamedly using the court as a forum to air all his unpleasant grievances about Mum and us. For the moment it looked as though we were going to have to be content just to know that he had been found guilty and locked up. We could worry about how long he was going to be away for later.

When the case was over the two barristers were chatting together. 'They'll be off for tea and scones now,' one of the policemen said wryly. It seemed strange to think that a case that was so traumatic and life-changing for us was just a job of work for them, something for them to chat about afterwards, comparing notes and discussing how it went as if it had been no more than a tennis match. There seemed to be an enormous distance between what was going on inside our heads and what we read in the papers or heard the professionals discussing around us. For us, this was about getting justice for Mum and also keeping Dad off the streets so he couldn't come after us seeking revenge for what we had said in court.

At the end of the whole proceedings the police told us we had been good witnesses. The fact that I had been unable to stop myself from blurting out in court once or twice didn't seem to matter because the judge even said something complimentary to us at the end, and then wrote us a letter congratulating us on how well we had behaved throughout the proceedings. He said he could see how hard it was for us to keep our mouths shut in the face of some of the things that were being said about us and about Mum.

It would be four years from 14th February 2003 – the day they pronounced him guilty – before Dad was finally given his tariff. Throughout those years we had no idea how long it was going to be before he was back on the street and able to come looking for us. I knew that everyone expected him to get a long sentence, but I had been let down often enough to know that you can never rely on anyone's opinion until it has been proved to be true. When I got the phone call from our victim liaison officer to say the paperwork had come through with the sentence, I was a university student working in a laboratory. I wasn't supposed to take calls in class but when I saw who was calling I answered it anyway, desperate to know that we were safe for a good few years yet.

'I've just got all the stuff from the Home Office,' she told me. 'His tariff has been set at ten years.'

I had been imagining he would still be in for a minimum of another ten years, maybe even twenty and I couldn't believe what I was hearing. That meant that with the time he had already served before coming to trial he might only be in prison for another five years – until January 2012. It seemed as though he might be back at any moment and Alex and I had no hope of any peace of mind.

We had been asked to fill out a victim's impact statement about a year before, which would be put in front of the judges making the decision about the tariff, but it had obviously had no effect on them whatsoever. It was likely that we would still be tied up with lawyers, courts and victim liaison officers, trying to resolve the financial issues between us by the time he came out. That meant we would never have a time when we were free of him. I had hoped there would be at least ten years after everything was settled when we would be able to get on with our own lives before we had to worry about him coming back out again to haunt us.

The length of the sentence just didn't seem to fit the gravity of his crime. As far as I can tell the minimum anyone can serve for murder is nine years. How could it be that the crime he had committed was only worth one year more than the minimum? Ten years might be appropriate for someone who attacked and killed another man in a drunken pub brawl, but is it an appropriate sentence for a man who allegedly sharpened his chisel in advance, which suggests that he premeditated the attack, had no apparent provocation from the victim and continued stabbing over and over again, long after any initial impulse to strike someone would have passed? Why did he then ring the police and admit what he had done, and fifteen minutes later deny that he could remember anything about it? If the court had decided he was in his right mind, it seemed to us that this was about as bad as a murder could be, so why wasn't the sentence reflecting that? The only way I could imagine that it could have been worse would be if he had gone on to murder more people, or had gone on the run rather than turning himself in.

Once Dad had been convicted of murder he could no longer inherit Mum's half of the house, because that would mean that he was benefiting from his crime, and so it automatically passed to Alex and me. But now that we knew the whole truth of what he had done and what he thought of Mum and us, we couldn't see why he should be allowed to keep the proceeds from the other half either. We knew that it had always been Mum who had worked in order to earn the money to pay the mortgage, so why should he have any claim to anything? Since he had deprived us of our mother and we needed all the financial support we could get if we were to continue our educations, as Mum would definitely have wanted us to, we felt he should be made to contribute from his share. So we went to the solicitor who had been helping us and asked if it would be possible to try to get things made fair.

The solicitor warned us that he thought by the time we had been through the whole fight, we probably wouldn't make any money from it, and if we lost we might even end up losing money because of the legal fees, but by that time it had become a point of principle – more about ensuring that he lost everything than that we gained any financial advantage. It didn't seem to us that Dad was really being punished for what he had done, since he had wanted to go to prison all the time anyway. Being shut in a cell and having all his meals provided for him, with no responsibility for looking after himself, is exactly how he likes to live. The thought that he would eventually come out and have a nest egg of money waiting for him, money that Mum had worked so hard for over so many years, didn't seem right. We were also suing Dad under the Fatal Accidents Act for depriving us of the financial support Mum would have continued to give us had she been alive, and for the psychological harm he had done us by killing her. The fight still goes on but the lawyers tell us that if we win we will be the first people ever to have sued a parent successfully.

By the time Dad's sentence was decided he had already shown that he was co-operating with the authorities; he had already served part of his sentence and the Home Office was worried about prison overcrowding. It was decided in some closed meeting somewhere that the only people Dad was a danger to now were Alex and me; he wasn't a danger to the general public and therefore wouldn't need to be locked away forever.

The thought that in a very few years he could be back out on the street is very frightening for us. He isn't allowed to know where we are, and we aren't allowed to know what prison he is in. In a way that is good, but we're worried that if we don't even know what part of the country he is in we might bump into him accidentally once he has been released. Helen is frightened of him coming out as well because she stood up in court in front of him and called him 'Mad Bert', saying how much she hated him. She had told the police all about him during her interviews, when she was still too upset to think through the possible long-term consequences of anything she might say. I dare say she would not have been so bold if the police hadn't already got her words on tape. Saying it out loud when she was just a few yards away from Dad was a very different matter to saying it to a couple of friendly policemen in the security of a cosy police station, probably with a steaming cup of tea in her hand. She had been the witness with the most to say, and she knew it wouldn't be hard for Dad to find her if he decided he wanted to get his revenge once he was out. In the few times I've seen her since the sentence was set, she has professed to be very worried about what Dad might do when he comes out, and I'm not surprised. We all are.

Chapter Seventeen

Alex

Isobel and I lived with Cathy and Pete for twenty months in the end, from March 2002 to November 2003. Exactly a year after we got there Alfie died of leukaemia – again on the 11th, a date that seemed to bring us one disaster after another. It felt as though we had lost an old friend and ally but we were used to absorbing blows like this without great shows of emotion, having been hardened to such things over the years by Dad killing our hamster and rabbit. Cathy and Pete couldn't understand why we weren't crying about it.

'If we didn't cry when our Mum was murdered,' Isobel pointed out, 'we're hardly going to cry over a dog.'

It seemed the foster parents were more upset than us, which led to some tension.

'They don't even care about their own dog,' we heard them say when they thought we were out of earshot, 'so why should we bother doing anything for them?'

It was just one more blow that we had to cope with, not something to make a big fuss about. From the beginning I think both Isobel and I had coped pretty well with everything fate had thrown at us, and we had done it by taking each day as it came, overcoming each obstacle as it appeared. Most of the responsibility fell to Isobel because she was the older of us, and the more outspoken. Some of the people we came across in the system were really helpful, although they never had enough time to do everything that they might have wanted to do for two children trying to organise their lives on their own. The good ones always seemed to be worked off their feet. There was a family protection officer called Stella who gave us a lot of her valuable time and chatted to us about any issues that were worrying us, and the two CID officers who interviewed us the first day after the murder were really conscientious about keeping us abreast of what was going on behind the scenes. But the good people only have a limited amount of hours in their days, and as it became increasingly obvious to everyone who knew us that we were doing fine at school, and that Isobel was there to help look after me, we heard less and less from everyone in authority, until we eventually reached a situation where I never even got to meet my social workers at all.

About six months after Mum's funeral, in August 2002, it suddenly occurred to us that we had no idea what had happened to her ashes. Isobel asked our foster parents where they thought they were.

'You haven't had them yet?' they asked, obviously surprised by the revelation.

They made some enquiries and discovered that the social workers on our case hadn't collected them from the crematorium after the service as they were supposed to. Because there had been no one to chase them up, they had disappeared into the system. It seemed the final insult to Mum's memory and Isobel demanded that something should be done. She was beginning to get very good at standing up to grown-ups and not allowing them to patronise us when we felt strongly about something. They instigated a search and eventually managed to track the urn down for us so that we could arrange to have the ashes buried and we would know that Mum was finally at peace. We never seemed to reach any sort of closure on anything. We just wanted to put our childhoods behind us so that we could concentrate on looking forward instead of back, but there always seemed to be so much unfinished business hanging over us.

We found a nicely kept graveyard in Redditch, which we thought Mum would have liked, and commissioned a headstone with the little bit of money left over from the collection Jillian had taken at Mum's school to pay for the funeral. We held a short ceremony at the graveside with a priest saying a few words. It was very small and private, completely different to the crowd at the funeral, most of whom can hardly have known her at all. The group around the grave included all the people whose lives had been truly affected by Mum's passing. Helen brought one of her sons, the first time we had seen her since we were taken away to Cathy and Pete's, but she only stayed for about ten minutes so we didn't have time to talk.

Cathy and Pete were there too, which didn't feel quite right to Isobel and me, especially when they threw some dirt into the grave in what seemed like an overly familiar gesture. Maybe I was being too critical because by then I already knew I didn't like them, but I kept thinking that they had never known Mum and didn't have a good word to say about the way she had brought us up, so why were they now standing side by side with the people who had loved Mum? I didn't say anything, as usual, but the thought simmered away inside my head.

I suppose they felt they were supporting us, which was part of their job. They had all sorts of ideas about what we should do and how we should behave, none of which we were very receptive to. They tried very hard, for instance, to make us look on them as our natural parents, wanting to integrate themselves into our existing family, even though our family were all strangers to us. They insisted on taking us to meet Mum's cousins, who we had never met before, and they stayed in contact with them after we stopped living with them. They all discovered they had a common interest in drinking wine, a pastime that didn't interest Isobel or me in the slightest.

Just after the burial of Mum's ashes, they agreed to take us back to our family home so we could pick up more of our stuff. At that stage Dad had still not been convicted so the house was legally his. We had been asking for ages if we could go there but the police had been adamant that no one should be allowed into the crime scene, even though they must have found every clue they could possibly need within a week or two of the murder.

We were grateful to Cathy and Pete for giving in to us because they weren't supposed to do it, but I expect they were curious to see where we had come from, having heard so much about our past. Even though the police had forbidden us to go back to the house, no one had thought to take our keys away so it was easy to walk in now that the police no longer had anyone guarding the premises.

It was an eerie and disturbing feeling to open that front door again seven months after the day the policeman told me to stay outside; we stepped back into a ghost house full of memories. Our lives had changed completely since we were last there, and we had had to adapt too. The house smelled terrible because the electricity had been turned off but food had been left to rot in the fridge and on the shelves in the kitchen. A pint of milk that had been left curdling by the sink, some bananas had blackened and turned to ash in the fruit bowl, and wet clothes had been left to rot in the washing machine. It still looked the same, every room bringing back a host of memories and painful emotions, reminding us of what it had been like to live there with Mum, resurrecting the feelings of fear and hatred of Dad that had smouldered beneath the surface all through the years that we had lived our lives within those walls.

Someone had obviously done their best to clear up the bloodstains by the back door, but they had found it impossible to get rid of every trace and we could see reddish brown smudges on doorframes and in corners where it hadn't been cleaned off completely. There were lots of arrows that the forensic team had stuck up all over the place in order to help them identify where the blood had been. There was no question that we were visiting a murder scene as well as the place that had been our childhood home.

We walked through like tourists initially, staring at everything, taking it in, trying to work out what we were feeling. Were we sad or angry? I suppose we initially had that feeling of emotional detachment that the psychologist had explained can result from severe shock. We climbed the stairs and came to Dad's closed bedroom door. All our lives we had been walking past that door, wondering what was going on behind it, whether he was there or not. We didn't say anything, because we both knew the other was thinking the same thoughts. For the first time ever we could be absolutely certain he wasn't in there, but we were less sure if we wanted to go in. After a few seconds' hesitation, we made up our minds and pushed open the door, stepping into Dad's secret inner sanctum for the first time ever. Whenever he went out he had always locked the door behind him, keeping the key on a chain around his neck. It was like an alien landscape, a dingy home within a home, a squalid little bed-sitting room. It was hard to imagine how he could have borne to spend so much time on his own in such a dreary, self-contained bunker. We just stood there, staring around us at his television and his computer screen, and the few kitchen appliances he had kept in there so he could make himself drinks and simple meals from tins without venturing out and risking bumping into any of us. It was as if we had entered the camp of a hated and now defeated enemy and our initial trepidation, instilled by years of his tyranny, deserted us to be replaced by a mindless fury.

All at once, we both went mad with rage. We started throwing things around the room, cutting up Dad's clothes with a pair of scissors and messing everything up, as if we could somehow punish him for what he had done to us, even though he was locked up and miles

210

away. There was no logic to our rampage; it was just a gut reaction to a man who had been so vile to us for so long and had finally robbed us of our mother, our roots and our family.

I ran down to the garage and grabbed a can of spray paint. Cathy and Pete asked what we were doing, but we ignored them. Isobel and I took turns to spray-paint the word 'murderer' on the wall downstairs and then all over the walls of Dad's bedroom. There was a feeling of liberation as we let all our bitterness and anger out, while our foster parents stood by, looking on grimly, saying nothing. Maybe they were pleased to see us rejecting our past life like that; maybe they realised it was an emotional release. Eventually we had spent all our energy and anger and we collected the things from our rooms that we had come for.

As we came back downstairs we noticed that the message light was blinking on the telephone and when we pressed the button we heard a male voice with a Scottish accent. He announced himself as being somebody 'Kerr', so we assumed it was a relative of Dad's, but it wasn't a name we recognised. The voice asked if he was still planning to come up to Newcastle, so news of what had happened can't have travelled that far. It was unusual for Dad to receive any phone calls at all, and we had never ever heard him speak about his family so we had no idea if this was one of his brothers or a cousin. We might as well have been listening to the voice of an alien. The police had never mentioned the message so the man must have called after they had left the house. Isobel and I wondered if Dad had maybe been planning to run away after killing Mum and had contacted this 'Kerr' to see if he could go there, but had later thought better of it. We have no way of knowing for sure.

The police must have gone back for something after our visit and found the mess we had made. They realised immediately that we were the culprits because of what we had written. Once we had calmed down, we began to worry that in our anger we had made a mistake and given Dad an opportunity to press charges against us for damaging his property. It was still his house at that stage. The police came to warn us not to do it again and took our keys off us but fortunately nothing else happened. It seemed strange that we weren't allowed to do whatever we liked in a house that had been our home for so many years but they were adamant we had to stay away.

Eventually the house was sold. I think Dad's solicitor took care of the sale, and we managed to get our share of the money out of him after Dad was convicted, so that we would have a deposit to put down on a house of our own later. I don't know who bought it. I wouldn't have wanted to move into a place that had been the scene of so much unhappiness, pain and horror, but maybe the price was so low someone was unable to resist it. It made us really angry to think that Mum had worked so hard for so many years, paying every instalment of the mortgage and every household bill, while he just sat in his room, hating her and resenting everything she did, and then he ended up getting half the house. The lawyers tried to explain to us that he wasn't technically 'benefiting' from his crime because the house was already in his name, but none of their arguments seemed morally right.

The guardian ad liteum we had been allocated by social services, a woman named Marjorie Woodford, was supposed to look after our best interests, coming up with an education plan and advising on where we should live. Isobel and I liked her because she asked direct questions and was a no-nonsense type. Quite early on, she wrote a report saying that she didn't think our foster parents were suitable for us but social services didn't take any notice. As far as they were concerned, Cathy and Pete were doing lots of nice things for us like taking us on holiday, so they assumed we must be happy to be with them. After a while, however, other people started to question their suitability for the job too. The school wondered why they never bothered to turn up for parents' evenings, and people outside the school wondered why we weren't doing any of our activities any more when we had been so keen and conscientious in the past. We kept hoping that the authorities would decide they needed to move us to someone more suitable, but the months continued to pass without anything changing. The worst part of having your life run by bureaucrats is that you never know what they are doing. Were they working away behind the scenes in our interests? Or had they forgotten all about us, assuming we were okay so they could get on with more obviously pressing cases? We had no way of knowing. All we could do was wait and see what happened.

Cathy began to get feedback from her social worker suggesting that she and Pete were not doing their fostering job properly, which fed the resentments in the house. They didn't like being criticised when they believed they were doing us a favour by giving us a home at all. They were convinced they had gone into fostering with the best intentions, but it certainly wasn't working out the way they had hoped and they believed that was our fault. They had real trouble disguising their annoyance and disappointment with us. In retrospect it was inevitable that we were all heading for some sort of explosion.

Chapter Eighteen

Isobel

Cathy and Pete must have been becoming more and more disillusioned with us as the months went past and we didn't become any more affectionate towards them, or gushingly grateful to them for agreeing to take us in when no one else wanted us. The ill feeling between us was building all the time but the first major explosion came when I brought a girlfriend called Tania home from school. She was having difficulties with her family at the time – her stepdad was beating her up – so she was staying with us quite often and no one had ever said it was a problem.

That particular evening Cathy and Pete had had a lot to drink and had gone to bed before us. I don't think we were doing anything very bad, but we hadn't gone to sleep as early as we might have done, wanting to lie in bed and chatter the way that teenage girls do. We must have been laughing too loudly because we woke them up or stopped them getting to sleep or something that lit the

215

touchpaper and ignited every little pent-up resentment they had stored up inside them.

They exploded into my bedroom, ranting and raving at us to such an extent that we became frightened. It was like suddenly being thrown back into one of the worst rows at home and I just couldn't face it. Alex woke up and came running from his bedroom under the impression that we were being attacked. We both felt we couldn't deal with things and had to get away. The three of us, desperate to escape from what seemed like a very real threat of violence, hurriedly packed our things and ran out of the house. Even though it was the middle of the night we had to take Tania with us since we could hardly leave her on her own in the house with them when they were behaving so weirdly.

Once we were out on the streets in the dark there was nothing for us to do but to keep walking, hoping that something would occur to us. Our foster parents must have called the police almost immediately we left the house, and it didn't take long for them to find three lost-looking teenagers wandering around the deserted streets. They took us back to the police station first, to try to find out more about us and about what had happened to cause us to walk out into the night like that. They were very friendly, just as they had been when we were first interviewed after the murder. We even watched them playing pool for a while as they tried to work out what they should do with us.

Although we had no idea what the alternative might be, we begged them not to take us back to the foster parents. We explained that they were always drunk and that we didn't feel safe in their care, but in the end the police decided they had no option since they didn't want to put us in the cells for the rest of the night. Remembering my failed and short-lived shoplifting career, I was quite glad that we didn't have to go through that, although it wouldn't have felt so threatening with Alex and Tania there.

Eventually we realised it would be fruitless to argue with them any more. If there was one thing we had learned over the previous year and a half, it was that people like us had very little power to change the minds of those who decided our destiny. We could tell them we didn't want to go, that we were frightened, but ultimately the decision would be theirs.

When we got back to the house Cathy and Pete were waiting and they were absolutely furious. As well as being kept awake they had now been made to look like bad foster parents and they were not in a forgiving mood. With folded arms and angry tone, they told our police escorts that they didn't want us back in their house. I guess they'd had enough of us by then and had decided that even if the money was good, fostering a couple of ungrateful teenagers wasn't worth all the grief.

'If they come back here we are going to end up hitting them,' Cathy warned grimly.

To the police I suppose it must have looked like a normal falling out between teenagers and their parents. Maybe they're called out to such incidents all the time, and they didn't know what to do with us in the middle of the night anyway, apart from put us in the cells, so they talked to us all separately until they were satisfied everyone had calmed down a bit then they left Alex and me there and took Tania back to her own family. I don't know what they would have done if Cathy and Pete had actually attacked us once they'd gone.

Because the police had been involved, social services were forced to react and they came round to see us the following day to try to find out what had gone wrong. Cathy and Pete hadn't relented at all and made it clear they wanted nothing more to do with us. We said, as politely as we could since they were in the room with us all the time we were being interviewed, that we would also like to leave. Looking back now I wonder if they were keen to get rid of us before we were taken away from them, but didn't like to say. Maybe they thought it would have looked bad on their record – a bit like resigning from a job before you get fired.

But it wasn't going to be that easy for any of us to escape the situation. It had taken social services a lot of effort to find this home for us, although we didn't realise it at the time. It was going to be even harder to find another placement now that the relationship had gone wrong and future potential foster parents would be able to read on our record how troublesome it had turned out to be. It seemed we had no option. We were going to have to stay where we were for the foreseeable future and just make the best of it. Now that Cathy and Pete knew we wanted to go too and that there was no chance they were ever going to be able to turn us into the loving little family unit they had imagined when they agreed to take us on, it became all-out war.

'I'm not surprised your dad killed your mum,' Cathy announced brutally in the middle of one of our many disagreements, 'with children like you.'

It seemed that in her opinion we were such terrible children we had driven our father to murder our mother, which was pretty much what he had claimed in his defence in court. How could any child be that bad? Her words hit a raw nerve with both of us and we weren't sure how to cope with the feelings of anger that welled up. We still hadn't had any bereavement counselling and we were finding our emotions hard to cope with. I'm not sure why nothing had been organised by then. Initially we had been forbidden counselling until Dad's trial was over, in case we had ideas put into our heads that would jeopardise the chances of him getting a fair hearing. Afterwards I think everyone just forgot because so much time had elapsed and because we seemed to be functioning okay at school and not getting into any trouble apart from rowing with our foster parents. Even then, the rows can't have seemed particularly serious to the police or the social workers compared to the sort of violence they were used to seeing in dysfunctional families. Mostly we were just quiet and distant and not interacting with them as they would have liked. As always our main strategy was to suppress all our anger and anxiety and get on with the daily business of our school lives as best we could.

There was part of us that knew it was ridiculous to say we had caused Dad to kill Mum, but at the same time the words rattled us and stirred some deeply buried feelings of guilt. In our darkest moments we couldn't help but wonder if maybe we should have done more for Mum. Maybe we should have gone to the police more often ourselves, and told them exactly how dangerous we thought Dad was. But then we were used to living with him so he only seemed really dangerous at the moments when they were fighting. Maybe we should have tried harder to persuade her to leave him. If she had been staying mainly for our sakes, perhaps we could have convinced her that we would be okay if we moved out of the house. Maybe we would even have been better off. Could we have saved her life if we had acted differently in any of these ways? The doubts kept on nagging away at us but we had no one we could talk to about them apart from each other.

'Would you like us to arrange for you to talk to anyone?' Cathy and Pete eventually asked once the trial was over. It was the first time anyone had ever suggested that to either of us, and I couldn't see the point by then. Because we hadn't been allowed to have counselling before the trial, we'd got used to managing without it. We had survived through the most painful months immediately after Mum died, when the loss was raw, so why would we want to rake it all up again now? We knew all too well how horrible our home lives had been, so we didn't need to go over and over the gruesome details with some stranger in order to remind ourselves. It seemed to me it would be better to spend the time finding ways to improve our current situation and move forward rather than dwelling on the past the whole time.

'No thanks,' I said. 'I think we'll be okay.'

But they thought different. No matter how much we protested that we didn't need help, they were determined to try to make us show at least some sort of emotional response to everything that had happened to us. When we continued to decline the offer of counselling they told us that they would stop our pocket money if we didn't do as they suggested. Although it sounded a bit like black-mail it did the trick. Alex and I talked about it between us and decided we didn't think it would do any harm, even if it didn't do us any good. We certainly didn't want our pocket money stopped, so we agreed.

Alex went first. His counsellor was a man who had a smart office with nothing in it but chairs and a big plant. Apparently, with the kind of psychoanalysis he practised, you are not supposed to ask any leading questions but just let the patient raise topics if they want. He started by attempting to make a personal connection with Alex by broaching the subject of football.

'I see David Beckham's in the papers again today,' he said cheerfully.

But Alex didn't really know who Beckham was so that didn't get the conversation going. Changing tack, the counsellor started talking about the plant in the corner of the room, but that didn't get them too far either so they ground to a halt. Alex ended up staring out the window at some pigeons for half an hour until the session was over and he could leave having fulfilled his side of the bargain. Cathy and Pete managed to bribe him into going a couple more times before he finally dug his heels in and refused to go any more. Anything he had ever wanted to discuss he had talked about with me or with his mates over the previous two years. He's never had any trouble saying whatever he wanted to his

222

friends, quite a few of whom had known Mum from our activities. His friends even came to him with their problems, knowing that he'd been through a lot himself and would understand more than most people of his age. He couldn't see the point of talking to a perfect stranger about anything.

So I had an idea what was in store for me when it came to my turn. I went in and sat down with the posh-sounding lady I had been allocated.

'You've got an hour to say whatever you want,' she informed me.

I went to eight or nine sessions over the following few months but I never really said anything about any of the worries or bad memories that were stored in my head. I didn't mind talking about things that were worrying me that day or that week, but I didn't want to go over all the old stuff that we had already been over in court and with our foster parents and in our own memories a thousand times.

Alex and I both had plenty of friends at school, even though it was harder to stay in touch with them now we lived so much further away. We didn't tend to use our time with them to delve into our emotions, though; we preferred to escape from our own thoughts when we were out with our friends.

Just after my seventeenth birthday, I got my first proper boyfriend, a boy from school called Martin. He came to the house to stay over for weekends and Cathy and Pete didn't have any problem with the relationship. I guess most parents of teenagers have a dilemma about where to draw the line, unsure whether to be strict and risk alienating their daughter or to be liberal and risk things getting out of control.

But then the thing happened that must be every parent's nightmare, as well as every teenager's – I discovered I had got pregnant. Martin and I had thought we were being really careful and sensible but we took a risk and didn't use a condom just one time, and that was enough. I couldn't believe my bad luck. When the tell-tale symptoms started to arrive I took about ten pregnancy tests, unable to believe my eyes when each one told me the same thing. Positive! I was showing my friends and even poor Alex. He really didn't want to have to think about his big sister in that way but he was my only family and my closest friend by then. We had been through so much together I couldn't have kept this latest development from him.

As the inevitable truth dawned on me I was horrified, partly because there was no way I was ready to have a baby, and partly because I knew it would reinforce the idea that it was us – or at least me – who was the problem in the fostering situation rather than Cathy and Pete. I had conformed perfectly to the stereotype of the damaged child from the dysfunctional background. I had always intended to go to university in order to fulfil all the potential that Mum had worked so hard to bring out in me and becoming a single teenage mum was definitely not part of my life plan.

I was in such a panic when all the tests kept coming up positive that I went to Cathy to confess, even though we weren't getting on well at all by then. She took me to see the doctor, who did another test and confirmed what I already knew. I couldn't keep up the denials any longer. The question then was what options were open to me? I felt instinctively opposed to abortion, not so much because of my religious upbringing but because it seemed wrong to kill a baby just because it wasn't convenient for me to have it. Even with the risk of Huntington's hanging over the unborn child, I felt that emotionally I couldn't agree to a termination. Both my foster parents, however, saw this as the simplest and most expedient way out of the mess and tried to talk me into it. Cathy and Pete were almost as embarrassed as me, believing that it reflected badly on them for allowing me to have a boyfriend in the house, and they just wanted the problem to go away. My stubbornness, as they saw it, served to widen the gap between us even further.

Now that Cathy and Pete knew, and the doctor knew they knew, there was no way we could avoid informing social services of this latest development. When they heard, they were annoyed with Cathy and Pete for letting Martin stay over so much, believing it was irresponsible of them. The social workers then started putting pressure on me, telling me that if I didn't agree to a termination I would have to go to a 'mother and baby' unit. They made the whole thing seem very threatening, but I still wasn't willing to consider an abortion. As far as I was concerned this baby had as much of a right to be born as any other.

The worst thing about the pregnancy would be that it would make it harder for me to stay with Alex and keep an eye on him because I would have to do what was best for the baby as well. In many ways I had taken over Mum's role in making sure he worked hard and didn't let any of the advantages she had won for him slip through his fingers. I wasn't sure that he was quite ready to be left to his own devices by then – he was still only fourteen – but if I had a baby to take care of I might not be able to look after both of them in the way I wanted to. I felt as though I was being torn in two, but I couldn't have said any of this to Alex for fear of making him feel guilty, as if he was a burden to me. He never felt like a burden to me because he was as much of a support for me as I hope I was for him.

I was about two and a half months gone when I woke up one night and found I was bleeding heavily. I was terrified and, not knowing what else to do, I went to

226

wake my foster parents, but they were too drunk to be able to offer any help. I just had to clear up the mess as best I could, having no real idea what was happening. I went to see the doctor the next day and he said it looked as though I had lost the baby in the night and that I should do a pregnancy test in a week to confirm it. After that Cathy and Pete began to voice their doubts as to whether I had ever been pregnant in the first place, accusing me of making the whole thing up. Cathy suggested that I had just invented a pregnancy as an attention-seeking ploy. I couldn't understand why she would say that when I had shown her some of the positive tests and had even been to the doctor with her to have it confirmed. It seemed to me that their arguments had no more logic to them than Dad's mad excuses as to why he had killed Mum.

Because I'd told Martin about the baby, the school called Cathy and Pete in to talk about the situation. By the time of the meeting I had miscarried and Cathy and Pete repeated their new story that I had made the whole thing up, so I was made to look like I was a liar in front of my form tutor, on top of everything else.

When the rumour got back to Martin that I had made up the pregnancy story he was, understandably, angry to think I might have lied to him about something so important. No matter how often I explained the whole thing to him and showed him the tests and offered to get the doctor to talk to him, there were too many seeds of doubt sown in his mind and eventually we split up over it. I wasn't that bothered because things hadn't been going so well anyway, but he was so upset he didn't turn up at school for a while.

I suppose it was only a matter of time before the tensions between Alex and me and the foster parents exploded again, and ironically the inevitable fireworks happened on Guy Fawkes Night. A friend of mine phoned me and as I was chatting to her I heard someone pick up the extension downstairs and start listening in. I thought they'd done it by accident, perhaps wanting to make a call themselves, so I sent Alex down to ask them to hang up. After I came off the phone, Pete started shouting at me 'Why are you always so rude?' I told him I didn't think I was rude; I just didn't want him listening in to my private conversation.

'It's my house and my phone,' he yelled. 'I can do whatever the hell I want. For being so rude, I'm taking twenty pounds off your pocket money.'

'That's not fair!' I complained, and he said he was taking another twenty pounds, so I complained again and he said 'That's another twenty.'

They were just heading out the door to go off to a firework party. Alex likes fireworks so he had agreed to go with them. As the three of them left the house I called after them, 'See you later.'

I didn't mean to say it in a sarcastic tone, but maybe everything I said to them sounded sarcastic by that stage. Whatever the reason, those three casually delivered words were the final straw for my foster father and he flipped, charging back into the house from the car, coming straight at me, obviously furious and out of control. Realising I was in danger of being hit I tried to slam the door in his face but I didn't manage it in time so I turned and ran into the living room and curled up on one of the chairs to protect myself from whatever blows were going to come. All the old fears I had felt when Dad was rampaging against Mum came flooding back. I immediately realised my mistake. I should have run through the house, or upstairs, or anywhere rather than allowing myself to be trapped in a corner, but it was too late to do anything by then. I just had to protect myself as best I could. He was beside me in seconds and as I peered up from beneath my raised arm I saw him lift his fist and I braced myself for the punch.

As his fist came down towards me there was a crash behind him and Alex was there, having run in from the car to come to my rescue. He pushed Pete off balance so his blow just swung through the air and he stumbled backwards into the kitchen before regaining his balance. He spun round and turned his anger on Alex, punching him hard. He might have been fat and out of condition but he was a grown man and Alex, still a skinny young

229

boy, was no match for him without the element of surprise on his side. Pete grabbed Alex by the throat and lifted him clean off the ground and onto the kitchen work surface. Alex was swinging wildly and managed to knock Pete's glasses off, causing his nose to bleed at the same time and incensing him even further. The fight had become frenzied, just as I imagined Mum and Dad's last fight must have been. I had to do something to stop it before it ended in tragedy.

I jumped up from the chair and grabbed the house phone, trying to dial the police despite my shaking fingers, but by that time Cathy had made it back into the house and she ripped the phone from its socket, exactly as Dad used to do during his fights with Mum, cutting us off from the outside world. For a split second my instincts told me to attack her, all the old fears rising to the surface, but I stopped myself just in time.

'I'm going to call them on my mobile then,' I warned her, but she started raining punches down on me, while Pete continued to hit Alex in the kitchen.

'What are you doing?' I screamed at her, unable to believe things had reached such a pitch. My words seemed to bring her to her senses and she paused for a moment. 'Look at him,' I said, pointing at Pete. 'He's going to kill Alex. You have to do something! Stop him!'

She must have realised I was right and that Pete was about to do Alex some serious damage, which would have opened him up to all sorts of consequences and possibly even criminal charges. There was also a risk that in the heat of the battle Alex would grab any weapon that might come to hand and lash out with even more disastrous consequences.

'Get off him,' Cathy shouted at her husband.

Apparently hearing her voice through the red mists of his anger he backed off and for a second I relaxed. The next moment Cathy swung round and slapped me hard in the face then kicked me in the shin. It was as if she was trying to provoke Alex into attacking Pete or her again. Maybe she thought that it would look better when the police came if she could say Alex had attacked first. I shouted at Alex to warn him not to rise to the bait and then I fled upstairs, followed by their angry shouts ordering us to get out of their house and out of their lives once and for all. They screamed that we were to be gone before they got back and then stormed out to the car, presumably to go to their fireworks display as planned.

We quickly grabbed our few most precious possessions and some spare clothes, stuffed them into our school bags and hurried out of the house, our hearts still thumping from the confrontation. There was no way we wanted to be there for a moment longer than we had to be. The terror of being attacked by two large grown-ups like that was, for us, compounded by the flashbacks it brought on to all the horrible fights at home that had

231

culminated in our mother's murder. We were both shaking uncontrollably as we stumbled down the road, with no idea where to head for next.

Chapter Nineteen

Alex

It was a huge relief to get out of Cathy and Pete's house, even though we didn't have a clue where to go next or what would happen to us. We realised once the adrenaline had settled down in our systems that we were hungry and went for a takeaway burger with the cash we had in our pockets. I was feeling, and looking, pretty bruised and battered at that stage but eating made me feel a bit better about life. Surely the authorities would have to do something to help us after this? The police wouldn't be able to just send us back to them now that they had attacked us physically.

Once we'd eaten we still weren't any further on with our plans; we just knew we didn't intend to go back to the house, no matter what. It was cold so we had to keep moving in order to stay warm. We had imagined some-one would have come looking for us by then, just as they had the last time we'd run off in the night, and we weren't sure what to do next. What if Cathy and Pete had decided not to ring the police this time and were just going to let us go? Even though I was still only fifteen, Isobel was seventeen by then, so maybe they thought we were old enough to survive on our own. But if that was the case we hadn't got the faintest idea where to start.

The twenty-four-hour Tesco store was the only place we could think of that would still be open, other than pubs and restaurants, and we didn't have any more money. We walked to the supermarket and sat on a bench outside, not wanting to attract any attention by going in but feeling a little safer for being close to people, hoping that something would happen or we would come up with an idea of what to do.

A few hours later Cathy and Pete's social worker rang Isobel's mobile. To begin with Isobel didn't want to tell her where we were, unsure whose side she would be on, but eventually she gave in and at three o'clock in the morning a duty social worker turned up at the store to collect us. For those few hours we had pretty much become street kids. It was frightening to see how easy it was for young people's lives to slip over the edge into chaos.

Straight away she could see the bruising on my face from Pete's punches so she realised she couldn't return us to the house. She drove us to a place which she said was an 'emergency foster home'. We were let into the house by someone who had obviously been woken up to deal with us, shown to some bunk beds and told to go to sleep.

'You'll be picked up at six,' the social worker told us, 'to be taken to school.'

We were quite surprised that they wanted us to go to school after such a traumatic night, but I suppose the alternative would have been that we were hanging around their offices all day while they tried to work out what to do with us. On balance, I think I would probably have preferred not to go in that day. It wasn't that I minded going to school, but it had been a long, hard night and I could have done with a few more hours' sleep.

I was still doing my GCSEs at that stage, with Isobel pushing me very hard. Unlike her I wasn't a natural academic. I preferred subjects that were more hands-on and vocational. Isobel was very strict with me about doing my homework, just as Mum had always been, so I never fell behind but it was a struggle some days. Grown-ups sometimes used to tell her to lighten up on me, warning her that she was putting too much pressure on me, as if they were worried I might crack under the strain. But she knew what I was capable of and, just like Mum, she was determined that I wouldn't miss out on any opportunities in life just because I was finding the work a bit difficult and it would have been easier not to bother. I think some-times other people worried that she put too much stress on herself by taking responsibility for me as well. Some even suggested that it would be better for her if we were separated so that she could concentrate on her own life a bit more and let other people worry about me. But she had no faith that anyone else would keep on at me in the way she did, and she was probably right.

Until shortly before the fight we'd had an experienced social worker, even though we hadn't seen her very often, but her bosses had recently taken her off our case because we were classed as being 'easy' to deal with. Our file had been passed on to a twenty-one year old trainee, a girl only four years older than Isobel. She wasn't on duty that night so it was Cathy and Pete's social worker who turned up for us at six the following morning, after we'd only had three hours' sleep.

In our haste to pack and get out of the house we hadn't thought to pick up any of my school uniform so I had to go to school in the clothes I had been wearing on the streets the night before. It was alright for Isobel because she was in the sixth form and didn't have to wear uniform. We had hardly walked through the door before I was told to report to the headmaster. They kept a skanky spare uniform on the premises that was usually given to the naughty kids who deliberately turned up in their own clothes in order to flout authority, so I was given that – one more embarrassment that I really didn't feel I needed.

The other problem was that we were hungry because we hadn't had time for breakfast before being whisked away from the emergency foster home and we had no money left to buy anything to keep us going. We had tried asking the headmaster if we could have school dinners before because our foster parents hadn't been giving us lunch money. He had always refused permission, but we thought that on a day like this he would make an exception.

'Can we have a school lunch today?' Isobel asked him.

'No,' he said. 'Free dinners are only for people whose parents are on low incomes and social services are responsible for you.'

That, apparently, was the system and he wasn't about to make an exception, not even on a day that was going as badly for us as that one was. In the end our friends shared their lunch with us or we would have been totally starving.

Our young social worker picked us up again at the end of the school day, accompanied by our previous, more experienced one. The trainee must have been finding the whole thing overwhelming and realised she was out of her depth. It seemed ironic that we suddenly had two social workers at once, although we had often had periods when we had none at all for months on end. It was hard to build up relationships of mutual trust in such circumstances or to feel that any of them really knew much about us. They drove us back to Cathy and Pete's house to get the rest of our stuff, including my school uniform.

'We have no idea where we are going to place you tonight,' they admitted as we climbed into the car. 'We've been searching all day and there's nowhere for you.'

That was not what we wanted to hear, but there were other things we had to do before we tackled the accommodation problem anyway. Back at the house, we each packed whatever we could carry into one bag while Cathy and Pete sat in the sitting room downstairs and the social workers hovered between us to avoid any confrontations.

After we left the house, they took us to see a nurse to have my bruises looked at, although they still hadn't come up in their full glory yet. She also treated the bruising on Isobel's shin, where Cathy had kicked her. The evening was wearing on and there still wasn't anywhere for us to go to. The longer it took to find us somewhere to go the more nervous we became that we would be sent back to the foster parents just because they couldn't come up with an alternative.

'Don't worry,' they assured us when we told them our worries. 'You're not going back there, and they won't be allowed to foster again or work with children in any capacity.'

That was a massive relief to us. We were pleased to see that we were being believed for once and action was being taken. I suppose the bruises were evidence enough, but we were so used to nothing being done when we made a complaint that we'd learned not to expect anything.

When they realised we hadn't eaten properly all day the social workers took us to McDonalds for a meal, still having no idea what they were going to do with us afterwards. They were worried about what time they were going to get home themselves by that stage. I suppose they couldn't really leave us till we were safely housed and it would certainly be against the rules to take us home with them. There were times when we could see why individual social workers ended up feeling overworked and under-appreciated. It can be a thankless job.

After a lot more phoning around they finally found us places in a children's home that took new residents at short notice.

'It's in Cheltenham,' they told us. That was even further from our school than Cathy and Pete's had been, but at that stage we didn't feel we could complain.

The trainee drove us for about forty-five minutes to get there and went in with us. She looked so young the people running the home actually thought she was the one who was looking for a place to stay.

'You'll only be here for two weeks at the most,' she assured us once that misunderstanding had been sorted out. In fact Cheltenham was to become our home for the next six months of our lives. Now we knew for sure that we had become 'children in care'; what we didn't yet realise was that from now on the world would view us very differently. Simply by having those two words 'in care' attached to our records we had been branded as low achievers. Basically we were now going to have to prove to the world that we weren't complete losers.

A few days later the police came to talk to us and asked if we wanted to press assault charges against Cathy and Pete. We did consider it but in the end we decided we had enough to think about and didn't want to get involved in another court case if we didn't have to. Since there was no danger of us being sent back there, or of them becoming foster parents again to any other children, we decided it would be sensible to let the whole assault thing drop. We really just wanted to be allowed to get on with our lives.

Chapter Twenty

Isobel

The poor social worker was obviously anxious to get back to her own home by the time we arrived at Cheltenham, so she was very happy to hand responsibility for us over to the staff there. She left, without telling the key workers at the home anything about how we had come to be in her care in the first place. For all they knew we could have been delinquents who had just burned down their family home or been found in a gutter somewhere selling drugs.

They took our details as soon as she had left, wanting to know all sorts of personal details.

'Any tattoos or piercings? Any other distinguishing marks?' Apparently they needed to know things like that so they would be able to put out a description if we disappeared during the night and the police had to come looking for us.

'Have you had those streaks put in your hair?' they asked me.

'No,' I sighed, used to answering this one. 'They're natural.' My brownish-blonde hair looked as though I'd had artificial highlights although I'd never used any product on it except shampoo! It had been like that since I was born.

We were so exhausted by then we just wanted to be shown where we could sleep and left alone. However, they insisted on itemising every single possession we had brought with us in case we accused anyone there of nicking stuff. Our social worker had put padlocks on our bags to help keep our possessions safe, something we had never had to worry about in foster care. It felt as though we were being processed into a prison, as though we had done something wrong rather than been the victims of an attack. The woman taking our details was quite pleasant and chatty and obviously had no idea what we had been through over the previous few days. Her job was just to fire the questions at us and fill out the relevant paperwork. Once she went off duty she was replaced by a night worker who seemed as if she had been in the job for years and believed she had seen and heard it all.

'You kids are all the same,' she told us. 'Don't think you're any different.'

She basically thought that any child who ended up in care was automatically thick and troublesome. We were too tired to protest so we just walked straight past her and went up to bed. We were each given our own rooms.

I fell asleep almost as soon as I climbed under the duvet, but I was jerked awake with my heart pounding a couple of hours later when the bedroom door creaked open and a dark figure tiptoed in and loomed over me.

'Who's that?' I demanded. 'What do you want?'

'Just a routine check,' a strange voice replied. 'Go back to sleep.'

No one had warned us that they would be checking up on us at regular intervals throughout the night. I don't know if they expected us to do a runner, or to try to hang ourselves from the light fittings or what, but it was a strange feeling to know that I couldn't rely on the privacy of that little room, not even for the few hours I needed to sleep. Although it was good to be away from the foster parents, it still felt as though we had taken yet another step backwards in life.

The staff at Cheltenham came and went in shifts, so the people who had signed us in the previous evening had been replaced by the time we woke up and went downstairs in the morning. Again, no one had warned us that would happen. In fact they hadn't told us anything really, so it was baffling to find new faces there when we went looking for some breakfast. And, of course, they knew as little about us as we did about them.

'You're dressed for school!' one of them said, looking shocked that we wouldn't be taking this opportunity to have a day off.

'We always go to school,' I replied. 'Why wouldn't we?'

'No reason, I suppose. Most of the kids here wouldn't bother.'

We didn't ask anything more. We just ate our breakfast and waited until our social worker turned up to pick us up. She was going to have to give us a lift for the forty-minute journey to school since there hadn't been time for the home to organise a taxi service for us.

By the time we got back to Cheltenham after school that afternoon, another shift of new faces had arrived and there were four other kids hanging around. Because our social worker had assured us we would only be there for two weeks I didn't see why I should make any effort to make friends with the others. There was no point if we were going to be moved on again so quickly. We'd hadn't been introduced to any of them anyway and it was quite scary coming into such an alien place, where they all seemed to know one another already and all stood around smoking and shouting most of the time. It was easier just to go to my room and do my homework. So for the next few days I kept myself to myself and only really talked to Alex, as usual. I felt lonely and missed Mum with a terrible aching in my chest.

The rest of our possessions were packed up and moved out of Cathy and Pete's by a private removal firm. There were twenty-three boxes altogether, but no one

labelled the individual boxes and it was only after searching them all that I realised out shared laptop computer
had gone missing. We made a complaint and requested
compensation from the storage company but it turned
out that a social worker hadn't filled out the forms
correctly so the claim was thrown out. We then applied
for social services to get us a replacement computer, but
they said it wasn't their fault that it had got lost. We
would have been able to claim for it from the storage
company if the social worker had filled the forms out
correctly but for some reason this didn't count. They also
said we wouldn't be needing a computer for long enough
to make it worthwhile, since we were close to the end of
our schooling. It was a very disheartening introduction
to the inhumanities of the care system, where rules were
rules and exceptions were seldom made.

After about a week at Cheltenham, Alex was coaxed
downstairs by the staff to watch a football match on the
telly and he began to talk to the others. Alex never had
any trouble making friends in new places, because he
was an easygoing character, happy to talk to anyone. By
the end of the second week it was obvious we weren't
going to be moving on anywhere just yet. I realised I
couldn't spend the rest of my life in the bedroom and
started to venture downstairs as well.

The home wasn't a big establishment, although it felt
big to us because we had only ever lived with two other

people at a time. There was an independent unit attached to the home as well, for people who were almost ready to go out into the world and look after themselves but were still under eighteen. Some of the others had police convictions for crimes like car theft and criminal damage, or just for petty things that they had done around the home. It was the management's policy to ring the police every time any of us did anything that was against the rules. I've come across other homes that have the same policy but I don't agree with it because it leads to kids getting criminal records too young, without having done anything serious enough to merit it. Once you have a criminal record it is yet another stigma that you have to live down for years. It's hard enough convincing someone that you're worth anything if you've been brought up in care; if you have a criminal record as well, the obstacles to getting good jobs become almost insurmountable before you start.

The police were always turning up at the home to carry out drug searches, making us all take our coats and jumpers off, and lift our trouser legs up. We were always under suspicion of trying to hide something from them. I had a feeling that most of those searches were illegal since there was never any evidence found that Alex or I had even touched drugs, let alone carried them around. Both of us have naturally dilated pupils, which we grew tired of having to explain every time someone accused us of being high. According to the Police and Criminal Evidence Act an officer does not have the power to search a person unless he or she has reasonable grounds for suspecting that they will find stolen or prohibited articles. As we were never found to be taking or possessing drugs there were no reasonable grounds for suspecting us, other than the fact that we were living in a children's home. The Act also states that before a search can legally commence the officer must make you aware of their name and the name of the police station to which they are attached, the object of the proposed search and their grounds for proposing to make it – none of which was ever done.

I suppose there was good reason for the police to be suspicious of the home in general since every drug dealer in the area seemed to target the kids there, hanging around outside the gates waiting to pounce. I guess it happens in a lot of places like that where everyone knows there are disillusioned kids who are able to get their hands on a bit of pocket money each week but have nothing in particular to spend it on. Drugs are always going to be tempting to people whose lives are shit, and there was a lot of peer group pressure. Kids were told they would be allowed to hang out with the local people they perceived to be cool if they did something for them, like steal goods that could be sold on easily. Often eager to please and wanting to belong, children in care are sometimes easy to lead astray. Drug use would be an inevitable result in many cases. It's like a vicious circle – lots of vicious circles, in fact, most of them overlapping.

The police searches would happen every few weeks and on one of them twenty officers turned up at once to search the building from top to bottom. Even though they never found anything on Alex or me, and the sniffer dogs they brought with them could never smell anything around us, they still wrote down all that went on during the searches and I was really worried that when I went to my first job interview the information would pop up on some computer somewhere telling people that I had been suspected of taking drugs. When your whole life is in the hands of other people you never know what is being logged on your records somewhere to come back and haunt you later. Lots of people worry about our 'surveillance society' but no one suffers from it more than a child who has come into the orbit of the state's care system.

A really nice male social worker took over our case and he seemed surprised by just how much had happened to us in our short lives, and amazed that no one had told us what other types of counselling were available after the first sort had failed. He was the first person who actually realised that our emotional needs might not have been met. By looking at the records he could see that the type of counselling we had tried before wouldn't work and he wanted to make sure we knew what other options there were. As far as he was concerned, he was surprised that we hadn't had a total emotional breakdown by that point.

I wouldn't want to give the impression that everyone in the care system is useless. Some of them are brilliant. There was one male key worker in the home called Paul, for instance, who had been in care himself, with whom Alex formed a very strong bond. Paul was probably the first adult who had achieved that with either of us since Mum died, and he helped Alex a lot by explaining more about the care system and how it worked.

There were several really excellent female key-workers at the home at the time as well. Vanda, Sandy and Jeanette were particularly helpful with my OCD problems and didn't become impatient and shout at me in the way that Cathy and Pete had. For instance, they could see that I got agitated in the evenings, when it came close to bedtime. The kitchen was always locked at night but they would unlock it for me so I could go round making sure all the plugs were turned off before I went to bed. If I didn't go through all those routines I would find it hard to relax and get to sleep. It used to annoy the other kids because they thought I was being allowed into the kitchen to eat something as a special privilege.

Vanda was good at recognising when I was feeling anxious and encouraging me to talk about my feelings. I spent many hours chatting to her about things and she helped me to sort out a few issues. Sandy and another key worker called Debbie were also amazing. Sometimes they realised I needed to get out of the home and they took me out for a drive so I could chat about any worries I might have. They made me realise it was all right to talk about my problems, although I still didn't want to dwell on past issues or go into detail about how much I missed Mum.

The people in that home were also good at treating Alex and me as two individuals rather two halves of one problem, which was how we had got used to being seen by the social workers who had worked on our case up till then. A lot of the time over the previous eighteen months the authorities seemed to assume that I would look after Alex and so they didn't have to worry as long as we had a roof over our heads. In the home it was different and it was helpful to have different people talking to us separately.

Because Cheltenham was only meant to be for short-term care, other kids came and went all the time so we didn't get to make any lasting friendships with any of them. At one stage all of them except one moved on and no one new arrived for a while, so the staff ratio became one to one, twenty-four hours a day. It didn't last long before new kids arrived but it was good while it lasted, more like being part of a family again.

no one listened

The care workers were very restricted in the punishments they could dole out to kids who misbehaved and sometimes it seemed a bit unfair to me that whenever a kid kicked off and made a fuss about something, the staff would just try to calm them down. Sometimes the other kids caused such a racket that we couldn't sleep at night. Basically it seemed to us they were getting away with misbehaving, while Alex and I never got any reward for keeping quiet and going to school each day. Although they were very nice to us in the home no one from social services ever asked if we needed anything or if there was anything they could do for us because we just got on with life and didn't make a fuss.

When Christmas came a month after we arrived at the Cheltenham, we sort of assumed that Helen and Steve would invite us to their house for the holiday. We had often spent Christmas with them before we went into foster care, when Mum was still alive, and we knew they had been told that we were no longer at Cathy and Pete's, but no invitation was forthcoming. One of Mum's cousins, who we had only ever met two or three times, kindly offered to have us for a few days, but he explained that there would be a lot of family members there who we wouldn't know. When we thought about it we decided that he was probably just being polite and that it would be better if we declined. We assured him that our godparents had invited us, so he wouldn't feel remotely

251

guilty. So in the end we were going to have to stay in the home while all the other kids went to relatives.

It was hard to get into the Christmas spirit under those circumstances, however hard the staff tried to make things festive for us. Exactly the same thing happened again the following year at the next home we were moved to. It would always be a time of year that would remind us of Mum's death anyway, and listening to other people making their Christmas family plans, full of excitement and optimism, would be painful for us.

Alex and I didn't have any spare money that year at Cheltenham, so we each bought the other a CD, which meant opening our presents took about twenty seconds. The staff had cooked us a Christmas lunch, but none of them ate it with us because they were saving themselves for their own family meals once they got home. We could see they were putting on a brave face for us but they were obviously wishing they were already at home as they watched us tucking into the food. We could understand that. After all, being with us was being 'at work' over Christmas for them. If there had been somewhere for us to go they might have been able to close the unit down for a few days and all enjoy the holiday. None of them would have been allowed to ask us back to their houses, even if they'd wanted to, because that would have been against the protocol and breaking the rules. They weren't even allowed to let us know where they lived. I suppose that was for their own protection in case a kid started stalking them or something. It was supposed to be just a job for them and they were not supposed to allow themselves to become emotionally attached to their charges. Any that failed to follow the rules and actually allowed their hearts to rule their heads would be severely reprimanded and maybe even sacked. I suppose the system can't be allowed to have a heart in case it gets broken.

Three months later it was my eighteenth birthday but I didn't feel like celebrating it at all. The main significance of the date was that I was now allowed to take the test to see if I had inherited Huntington's disease from Mum. I talked them into letting me take it a couple of weeks before my birthday, and the results came through a couple of weeks after. Sandy took me to the appointment and was sitting with me when the geneticist gave me the fateful news – the results were positive. I had the disease, just like Mum and just like my grandmother before her. Suddenly my options for the future were radically altered. To start with I knew I wouldn't ever want to have children now, because there was a fifty-fifty chance I would pass the disease on to them and continue it down the line after that, plus there was the fact that I might not be around to see them grow up and might end up being a burden to them. On the positive side, at least I didn't have to worry about saving for a pension because

I was never going to live long enough to need one. I would also not have been eligible to join the police or the army, had I wanted to, but that fact was more relevant to Alex, who at that time was thinking he might like to join the air force.

There were so many thoughts swirling around my head after I got the test results that I couldn't react straight away. The geneticist seemed more worried about the fact that I hadn't cried than she would have been if I had completely broken down. Why did everyone always want to see me bursting into tears about everything? To me it just seemed like one more thing to cope with, something I could do nothing about. Sandy took me out for a drive around the countryside after I heard the news, knowing that I wouldn't want Alex to see me upset and giving me the opportunity to talk in private if I wanted to. All I really wanted to talk about was how having the disease was likely to affect my chances of getting interesting jobs, and my biggest worry was how Alex would cope when I died, seeing as he would then have lost every single member of his birth family. I think perhaps the odd tear escaped down my cheeks as I thought of all the possible problems this new revelation would raise.

When we got back to the unit I told Alex my news in private and he didn't react either – so then they thought that maybe I hadn't told him, that I was keeping it from him to spare him the worry. But it was just that neither of us were particularly bothered. The staff started getting together all sorts of information about the illness for me, but I didn't really want to know. I was happy just to worry about it later and deal with the symptoms when they arrived. There didn't seem to be much point getting all worked up now when it might not strike for another twenty or thirty years.

'Any of us could be hit by a bus tomorrow,' I reminded them, 'but you can't worry about that every day, can you? But that's what you're telling me to do. I could waste my whole life thinking about how I might die, or I could just live every day to the maximum. There are a lot of people in much worse positions than me, people who are already disabled or have a debilitating disease. I can still live a perfectly normal life.'

It seemed like the obvious way of handling it to me.

After the diagnosis, I travelled down to a hospital in London where the doctors were keen to do tests on me because they didn't get to hear of many people my age who were known to have Huntington's. They told me that even if they found a cure for it they wouldn't know when to give it to me because they can't predict when it will start or what will trigger the onset. One day there may be a cure for Huntington's, they told me, perhaps even as a result of studying my progress, but I have to resign myself to the fact that it probably won't be in time for me to benefit from it.

no one listened

The rules surrounding friendships with care workers of any sort don't always work to the advantage of kids in care. Alex and I had to leave Cheltenham shortly after I got my Huntington's diagnosis, after just six months there. Vanda, Sandy and Paul were allowed to stay in touch with us for the first few weeks to help us to deal with the change, but after that we were supposed to stop contact. I think this is because they feel it would make it difficult for the workers in the next home to form relationships with us and to have authority over us. Vanda kept texting me for a couple of months but then she was told by her boss to stop it. I'm sure there are good reasons for these rules, but it is hard enough to form relationships with other people when you are in the sort of situation most of us were in, without having the ones you do form being artificially cut off every time you are moved somewhere new. It removed the possibility of forming normal, human friendships that could evolve over a number of years, as most good friendships do.

Sandy was able to stay in touch with me because she left her job soon after we were moved from Cheltenham, but I was surprised how much it hurt suddenly to be cut off from the other people I had grown close to, especially at a time when I was adjusting to a new home and a change of environment. It felt a bit like a repeat of the day when Mum died, as a large chunk of our previous life vanished completely overnight. Every time this

256

happened it reinforced the feeling that nothing and nobody can be relied on to stay with you forever. I made a conscious vow to myself that I wouldn't allow anyone in the next place to get so close to me, so I didn't have to go through the feeling of being separated from them again when the inevitable happened. I knew that I would soon be considered an adult and I would have to sever my roots again in order to move out into the world.

That feeling of needing to be self-sufficient in order to protect myself has stayed with me ever since. I try to do everything myself rather than ask other people for help, for fear that I will become dependent on them in some way. In my experience if you ever rely on someone else you end up being let down.

There are so many misconceptions about children like us who end up having to be taken into care, it is hard to know where to start when trying to dispel them. If ever you tell someone that you were 'in care' once you are out in the adult world their next question is nearly always, 'What did you do wrong?' The immediate assumption is always that you were taken into care as a punishment or because your parents couldn't control your behaviour in some way. I suppose in the old days Alex and I would have been able to say we went to an 'orphanage' and then everyone would know it was because we had lost our parents through no fault of our own, but no one uses that word any more. This stigma can have very real effects on applications for jobs and on forming relationships and any number of other life experiences. It marks you out as having come from a certain sort of background, a background that people assume makes it likely you are troublesome at worst and an underachiever at best.

If I don't want to go into the whole story behind how we came to be in care when I first meet someone, it's always best not to mention it at all. I read somewhere that only a tiny percentage of children in care (I think the figure was less than three per cent) are there through their own fault, but if you ask people to guess most would probably think the reverse was true. The vast majority of us find ourselves there because the adults who should be caring for us aren't able to. I would suspect that even that three per cent are misbehaving for a reason that is based on the way the adults in their lives have treated them. I'm not saying all children are innocent little angels; I'm just saying there are always reasons why they behave the way they do.

As long as I was still at school, or living in care homes, everyone always knew that I was the girl whose father had killed her mother. It had been our choice to stay in the school where the first big announcement was made at assembly, but the story would probably have followed us to any other school just because the teachers would have been informed and because the other kids would

soon discover we were in care and would want to know
why. At least by staying where we were we didn't have
to keep explaining ourselves because everyone already
knew the basic story.

The other drawback to people knowing about our
past is that it sometimes makes them reluctant to talk
about their own problems because they believe everything they say sounds petty in comparison to what we
have been through. It is hard to know which is the worst
option – not being able to talk about your past, or being
constantly judged for what happened to you years before.

Chapter Twenty-One

Alex

We were moved out of the Cheltenham unit a few days after Isobel was told she had Huntington's. In fact we had been due to move the next day but the key workers thought she might need a bit more support considering what she had just found out. As it turned out she was fine about it and didn't need any support, but even if she had been traumatised by the news I doubt if a couple of days would have made much difference.

The worst thing about being moved was that we lost touch with the workers who we had been getting on with so well – there was a guy called Paul I was very close to – and with the friends of my own age. I'd made a whole lot of new friends in the Cheltenham area over the previous six months because it's the sort of place where there isn't a lot for the young people to do so they just tend to congregate around the town centre together, talking. The locals were very wary of anyone they knew had come from the unit and if the community officer spotted us out and about he would always stop us and ask where we were going and what we were doing, as if we were bound to be off to do a bit of thieving or drug dealing just because we were in care. When we first arrived the people at the unit had warned us that they gave our pictures to the local shopkeepers as a matter of routine so they would be able to spot us and watch out that we didn't shoplift. I don't know if it was true or not, but it was depressing to think that we were automatically considered to be dishonest and untrustworthy just because we had ended up in their care.

Each place we were put into seemed to be further from our school than the last. This latest one was an independent unit attached to another home, which was progress for us, but it was an hour and a half's drive away. Trying to get to school from there by bus was virtually impossible. We were now cut off completely from our school friends socially because there was no way we could meet up with them in the evenings. You cook and clean for yourself in an independent unit, so Isobel was able to look after me on her own but she still had the staff of the attached home on hand for back-up if she needed them. Most of the time she was the most capable person on the premises anyway since she had been looking after our interests for over two years.

I was fifteen by then and Isobel had just turned eighteen. She never complained about having to look after me

– not that I ever needed much looking after compared to some of the kids we met in care. The only way in which she put pressure on me was in making sure I did my homework properly and going over any oral course work with me. The key workers sometimes worried that she was holding me back from developing my own powers of self-sufficiency by doing so much for me, but neither of us believed that. If Mum had still been alive she would have been doing even more for me, like most other fifteen-year-old boys' mums.

Whatever anyone said to us, we were always united in our determination not to be separated. If we hadn't got each other we would have had nothing at all at that stage. Although they believed Isobel should not interfere in my life as much as she did, when there was something difficult to do they would often ask her to do it for me. For example, after Isobel had left the home, they rang her when a worker I had bonded with died from liver failure and asked her to break the news to me because they thought I would take it badly and they didn't fancy telling me themselves.

While we were in the homes together they always had our review meetings together until the social workers and unit manager decided it would be better to separate us because I never got a chance to say anything. But they had misread the situation. The reason I never had anything to say was because I didn't have much respect for the people at the meetings or the things they were talking about. I believed I would be wasting my breath if I piped up. I've always preferred thinking to talking anyway; sometimes I over-analyse situations to a ridiculous degree. I've always been like this; if I haven't got anything to say I just keep quiet and wait for everyone else to have their say. Just because I'm quiet, however, doesn't mean I don't do a lot of thinking. Sometimes my brain is so busy I have trouble calming it down enough to let me get to sleep at night. It's always buzzing away, developing theories about anything and everything and exploring new possibilities. There had been so much in my childhood that I hadn't understood, and as I grew up I would sometimes get completely lost applying new discoveries to memories that had previously puzzled me. In particular, I kept trying to come up with logical explanations for all the sequences of events the day that Mum died. From time to time I would try my developing theories out on Isobel and she would pretty soon tell me to shut up.

'You're hurting my brain,' she would complain.

When they told us I must go to the next review meeting on my own Isobel was furious, aware that I wasn't as knowledgeable as her about the law and could easily agree to something that wasn't in my interests just because I couldn't be bothered to argue. I had to fill in a form before the meeting, which had a section asking if there was anyone I would like to accompany me on the day. They must have forgotten it was there, or thought I wouldn't notice. I just wrote Isobel's name in. Their faces were a picture of frustration when she came into the room at the beginning of the meeting with a copy of the form to wave at them when they asked her why she was there. There must have been times when we were very exasperating to them.

Isobel was due to leave school in a few months and was thinking seriously about what she was going to do next. She had gone off the idea of going to university when she did some research because the course she fancied – Forensic Science – was only taught at universities that were a long way away. I was going to have to stay in the home for a couple more years while I did my A levels and the thought of being separated by a big distance was hard for both of us. We both knew, however, that if she didn't go to university she would still have to leave the home and she would then have to find a job and support herself immediately, living in a hostel or a council flat or paying rent. That was what happened to most of the other kids we talked to in the home. The girls all seemed to think that getting pregnant and being given a council flat was probably the best option open to them and none of the staff tried to disillusion them and expand their horizons with alternative suggestions. When Isobel said she wanted to go to university the staff told her she was wasting her time because she was bound to fail, that she didn't have it in her and wasn't ready for it. No one seemed to think it would be worth trying to inspire kids like us to have higher expectations for our lives. No one thought to praise or reward us for going to school every day, for instance, in the hope that it would encourage others to follow our example.

I understand that it was difficult for the key workers because their powers of influence were limited. When kids in the home couldn't be bothered to get out of bed in the morning, the staff could hardly haul them out and drive them to school against their wishes, as a conscientious parent might try to do. Whenever we raised the subject with staff at the home they got defensive.

'It's all right for you,' they said. 'You have the work ethic because of how you were brought up by your Mum. Most of the kids here have come from families on benefits and they've never known anything else. That's all they aspire to.'

I don't think they realised quite how hard we'd had to struggle to keep going during the difficult times. Isobel and I thought that as corporate parents the staff at the homes should have been doing the same things for their charges that Mum had done for us, although Isobel tended to voice her opinions more often than me.

If she did decide to go on to university rather than stepping straight out into the world, social services would continue to pay her expenses and she would receive a small income from Mum's pension for as long as she stayed in full-time education. She would then be in a better position to do what she chose in life at the end of it. If she decided not to go she would immediately have to start earning a living and would be able to stay close to the home I was in, but she would lose the money from the pension. Although I think in her heart Isobel always knew that she should go to university and achieve the goals that Mum worked so hard to steer her towards, it was still a daunting prospect for her compared with staying in a familiar area and just getting a job.

She agonised over it for a long time but when she finally had to make the decision it was obvious that the right and brave thing to do was to go as far as she could with her education. Although I had always depended on her a lot, I had also learned to be pretty self-sufficient myself and I was sure I could manage on my own with the foundations that she and Mum had laid for me, and with the key workers from the home our unit was attached to for back-up. Plucking up all her courage, Isobel sent off application forms to six different universities, with no idea whether they would offer her places or if, as the staff at the home predicted, she was just setting herself up for rejection.

Over the following few weeks she was offered places at all six of them, much to the amazement of the staff. I felt so proud of her and sad at the same time to think that Mum would never know how all her hard work had paid off. No one in the care system seems to expect the children in their charge to go on to further education. None of the workers we came across had been to university themselves and none of the other kids felt that it was worth the struggle even to try to convince anyone of their potential. We knew just how hard it was to be taken seriously after we were unable to get a replacement computer when our own was stolen during the move to Cheltenham.

While we were in the independent unit the *Dispatches* television documentary team infiltrated a reporter into the home posing as a care worker, as part of a programme about the way children's homes in the area were run. It wasn't targeted specifically at our home because they took their hidden cameras to several others as well. The reporter befriended us and the other children in order to get us all to talk candidly, but they didn't show any of the footage they took of Isobel and me in the programme. I guess we didn't fit into the pattern of behaviour they wanted to illustrate. They wanted to show kids behaving in a disruptive fashion and illustrate how the system was letting them down but Isobel and I were just getting on with our lives as best we could in the circumstances, which didn't make for interesting television. We were in the room when many

267

of the conversations that later found their way into the programme took place and we knew that the editing process had frequently changed the sense of what was being said to make it more dramatic and in order to illustrate the points that the director wanted to make.

I suspect that some of the footage shown could have damaged the children featured in it. For example, it showed one child threatening to hit another over a stolen fag and a staff member saying, 'It's your fault if you get punched back.' It also showed some staff in the staffroom calling a particular child a 'slag'. It was true that not all the staff in the homes were brilliant, but the film actually made some of the good ones look bad and lost them their jobs as a result. The sacked staff then had to be replaced by agency staff who came and went very quickly and never formed any sort of lasting relationships with any of us. Many of the agency staff were foreign and knew nothing about the educational system in England and were even less able to advise us than the ones who had been sacked. On top of that some of the kids were all able to hear the staff talking about them on the programme via the reporter's hidden camera. Such conversations should have been confidential and hearing them broadcast undermined everyone's faith in the staff even more. We all knew they talked about us amongst themselves, but to actually hear them doing so on television must have been very unnerving for the kids involved.

Isobel had started taking driving lessons while we were living with Cathy and Pete, using her twenty pounds a week pocket money to pay the instructor. She took her test once we were in Cheltenham but failed it the first time because of her reverse parking. She didn't have any money left for more lessons so all she could do was rebook to take the test again, and hope for the best. This time she pulled it off. As soon as she turned eighteen, she got the money that our Granddad had left in trust for her and she decided to use it to buy a car.

When she told the staff at the new home that she was going to get a car, they laughed and said she would have to get a licence first. They couldn't believe it when she produced her licence and they realised that she had already organised it by herself. She was probably the first child in care they had come across who owned her own car. It was a wonderful feeling of freedom when she could finally drive us around and we didn't have to ask other people to do us favours by giving us lifts or bus or taxi fares all the time.

In October 2004, it was time for Isobel to leave the home and start university. It was a huge wrench for both of us, but at least now she had the car, she could drive back and forth to see me some weekends. It was a struggle for Isobel to manage financially without any parents to help, but somehow she still managed to bring me books to help with my A levels. She got a student loan but she had to pay all her accommodation costs out of that, which left her very little spare money from Mum's teaching pension to live on. She was also having to do all the practical things like buying toiletries and cleaning products and finding somewhere to live. Most students would be able to enlist their parents to help with at least some of these chores, but Isobel had to find out about it all as she went along, do it all herself and still make sure I was getting whatever I needed back at the home. I tried not to ask for too many things or to put her under any extra pressure but, like Mum before her, she was determined that neither of us should miss a single opportunity in life and that took an enormous amount of effort on her part. Lack of money was a constant source of worry. As long as I was in the children's home I was given twenty pounds a week to buy food (which meant I mainly lived on pasta and potatoes). The key workers would give me another ten pounds pocket money for myself, but I had nothing spare by the end of the week.

In the five years after Mum died, Isobel and I had thirteen different social workers, many of them kind people who were doing their best but just didn't have the time to do everything. When my last new social worker was assigned to me I met her once but at the time of writing, over a year later, have not seen her since. I know for sure that I would never have made it into higher education if Isobel hadn't pushed me to keep up my school-

no one listened

work at every opportunity. No social workers ever asked
me how I was doing at school, or what I wanted to do
when I left. As it turned out I suppose I have been okay,
but only because Isobel has been there for me at every
turn. She stepped into Mum's shoes on the 11th of January 2002 and has looked after me ever since. Life would
have been very different for me if I hadn't had her.

Chapter Twenty-Two

Isobel

Going to university was the first time that I had ever been separated from Alex for more than a few days. I'd accepted the offer from Staffordshire University and driving up on my own, having done all the preparation myself, was an overwhelming experience. I felt painfully lonely as I watched everyone else being dropped off by their parents, loaded down with pots and pans and various home comforts. The children's home had bought me one pan, one plate, a duvet and a pillow. Knowing nothing about university life it had never occurred to me that I would need all the stuff the others were carting in from their parents' cars.

In the following weeks, whenever I heard one of the other students talking to their parents on the phone, or watched them unwrapping a food parcel from home, I was reminded how alone in the world I was. I needed someone older and more experienced who I trusted to tell me that it was all right to feel the way I was feeling, but there was no one I could talk to since the people I had befriended at the first home weren't allowed to contact me. The only person I could turn to was my little brother, who didn't know anything about university life and had enough problems of his own to contend with. He suddenly seemed a long way away and I missed him badly.

Four weeks after the beginning of term I panicked, afraid that I was going to feel that lonely and unhappy forever, and I drove back to see him. When I got to the home I announced that I had made a mistake and that I was going to quit my course so that Alex and I could be back together again. When the staff at the home and the social workers heard they just smiled knowingly.

'We told you that you wouldn't be able to do it,' they gloated and there was nothing I could say in return.

Not one of them suggested I should go back and give it a proper go – Alex was the only one saying to me, 'Don't give up. You can do it!' But in the end I should be grateful to them because it was their negative comments that drove me to make the decision myself, just to prove them wrong. After two weeks of hanging around the home, listening to them and thinking through the consequences of my actions, I made up my mind to give it another go and got back into my car. Given time to reflect I realised that the alternatives to university were going to be much worse and that I would probably be feeling just as isolated in a council flat or a hostel some-where. At least at university I had a chance to make a new circle of friends and to get some better qualifica-tions. Once a child grows too old to be in care they have to go out into the world and fend for themselves as best they can. If they get a job and somewhere to live, that is probably as far as they will go. This university place was probably my only chance to go a little further.

Carol, a social worker I respected, once said to me: 'There are times when people in situations like yours decide either to sink or swim. You have obviously decided to swim.'

Her words kept going through my head as I drove back, determined to enjoy myself and make the best of the opportunities that were on offer to me. Even now, whenever I feel as though I'm struggling a bit, I keep telling myself, 'sink or swim, sink or swim.' It's funny how simple little phrases like that can sometimes seem to sum up all the wisdom in the world. I know that at low moments like the ones I experienced in those first few weeks away from Alex there must be many people who decide it is all too much of a struggle and just allow them-selves to sink. Maybe if I hadn't had responsibility for him as well as myself I wouldn't have been able to keep swim-ming for long enough to get through the hard times.

People often ask me if I chose Forensic Science as my degree subject because of what happened to Mum, but I don't think it was specifically that. I had always leaned towards the sciences, which probably was because of Mum's influence, but I knew my biology, chemistry and physics were not strong enough for me to do a pure course in them. I had always been interested in the idea of collecting evidence at crime scenes in order to get criminals convicted, regardless of what happened in our house that day, and when I discovered you could actually do a course on the subject it seemed like a useful and interesting thing to study.

One of the nicest things about going to university in a different city was that I could choose who I wanted to talk to about my past. At university, you can pretty much re-invent yourself and select which bits of your history you want people to find out about. No one knows anything about where you've come from or what your parents were like. It was a very liberating feeling. Once I had made good friends there, I would tell them bits about my background when the subject came up, but not until they had already got to know me for who I was, and weren't judging me based on the fact that my father had murdered my mother.

My biggest problem once I was at university was concentrating on the work. It was a standing joke amongst my friends that within five minutes of a lecture starting I would be off in my own dream world, thinking of all the things I needed to do to sort out my life and

Alex's: laying plans, compiling lists of phone calls I needed to make to solicitors or writing letters. I suppose that must have been what Mum's life was like as well, always working out how to get the two of us here, there and everywhere at the same time as doing her job to the best of her ability.

Luckily my lapses of concentration in lectures didn't matter too much because I've always been good at teaching myself. I did the same with my GCSEs and A levels, using the books to learn at home if I had missed a lesson due to attending the court case or talking to the police. There was one topic in a module that the majority of my class failed one year because the teacher had forgotten to teach it, but because I'd done it on my own without realising it hadn't been covered in class, I was one of the few who passed. The same happened at university. I found I didn't really need to concentrate in lectures because all the material could be found in the books or notes anyway. People often thought I was quite thick in classes and lectures because if a question was fired in my direction I would hardly ever be able to answer it. Sometimes I didn't even realise it was me they were asking and I would get told off for following flies round the room, my head in a complete dream world. But a month or so before the exams I would simply sit down and learn whatever needed to be learnt, blocking off whole twelve-hour days for revision and becoming frustrated if someone even walked near my room and their footsteps broke my concentration. I became totally stressed, worrying that I was going to fail and would end up letting everyone down, and wasn't able to talk to anyone for days on end. I couldn't bear the thought that I might not come out top of whatever I went in for. Then when the exams finally came round, a sudden calmness would descend. Studying that way had always got me top marks at school and the same happened at university. Everyone was amazed, including me, when I ended up being the only person who started the course in my year to be awarded a First.

If someone in care chooses to go to university the authorities will help them to fund it with grants and loans, but they will make no allowance for the fact that they have nowhere to go during the vacations. With the Christmas holidays looming at the end of my first term I realised that I wouldn't be allowed to stay in my room at the university, but I wasn't allowed to go back to the children's home either now that I had finished school. But I had no money to rent anywhere. I dare say a lot of people in that situation can find some relative or other who will take them in, but we knew from past Christmases that that wasn't a realistic expectation.

Fortunately for me, the home that Alex was living in applied for special permission so I could go back and stay with him during that first holiday. When they asked us what we were going to be doing on Christmas Day we explained we probably wouldn't be having a meal since we didn't have enough money to buy the ingredients. It didn't seem worth cooking a big meal just for two of us anyway, especially as I'm a vegetarian and Alex isn't, so they allowed us to come down to the home and eat lunch with the one other child who was staying over the holidays. They made it clear I could only stay a few days and it must never happen again.

When I returned during the Easter break, I still had nowhere to stay and so social services were forced to find me somewhere or see me homeless on the street. They responded by putting me into a bed and breakfast hotel. They dropped me off outside the place where they said they had booked me in. It didn't look too promising as I walked in but I was grateful just to have a roof over my head. As the first night wore on I soon realised my temporary home was a mixture between a brothel and a doss house. There were about six people sharing the bathroom and all the guests had to be off the premises during the day. The manager kicked us all out into the street at seven the following morning.

I hadn't slept well that night, after being forced to listen to the prostitutes working in the other rooms around me, and when I woke up that morning, which happened to be my nineteenth birthday, I decided I couldn't stay there a moment longer. I rang my social worker as soon as the office opened, but whoever answered the phone told me she was on annual leave and that there was no one else there who could do anything to help. Alex was still at school so the whole day stretched ahead of me with nowhere to go. Even once Alex was back at his flat I was only allowed in as a visitor between ten in the morning and ten at night. There was nothing else to do but sit in the car and wait for the hours to pass. So that was how I spent my birthday that year.

I could have filled those holidays more profitably by getting a temporary job of some sort but if I had done that I would have risked losing all the pension and social services money that I was living on during term time. The holidays were also only three weeks long, which limited the sort of jobs I could have done. I racked my brain for anyone I could contact for help, but I had lost contact with all my old school friends once I went to university, partly because I hadn't wanted to impose myself on them any more than I already had. Eventually I swallowed my pride and rang Helen, who I had hardly spoken to since Alex and I were put into the foster home, and I begged her to meet me in town. She eventually agreed but when I told her I needed help she was initially wary. In the end I begged so hard she gave in and reluctantly agreed that I could sleep on a pull-out bed in the office until term began again. Just having a roof over my head and not having to sleep in my car was good enough for me by that stage.

Although Helen let me stay for the holidays, I soon realised she was only doing it because she believed she had no choice. I felt as though I was in everyone's way and hated having to impose myself like that. She didn't trust me with a door key, so there was one night when I came back from seeing Alex to find she was out and I wasn't able to get into the house. I didn't want to cause a problem by asking them to come back early from wherever they were, so I slept in my car. The staff at Alex's home suspected what was going on and offered to let me stay in the staff accommodation, which was a kind gesture, but I turned it down. I was stubborn and didn't want to admit that I needed their help. In the end I told Helen I was going back to university earlier than I actually could because I felt so guilty about imposing on her, and I spent the last few nights sleeping in my car.

Even though I'd had so many offers from universities, had taken one up and was now doing well, social services still didn't believe Alex when we told them he was going to follow the same path. We had tried to find out in advance what sort of support might be available to Alex if he accepted one of the university offers, but the social workers wouldn't even discuss it, telling him it was a waste of time to think of it because there was no chance he would get in anywhere. When the offers started to arrive they had to think again and it was obvious they didn't have a clue where to start and were learning about it at the same time we were because the student loan system had changed so Alex's entitlements were different than they had been when I had started university.

As Alex's eighteenth birthday approached, we had a very important appointment to make. My heart was in my mouth as I helped him to make the arrangements to take his test for Huntington's disease. Surely fate wouldn't be so cruel as to let both of us have the faulty gene? If we had both had it, the chances were that I would be the first to die, just because I am older, and I worried about who would look after him once I had gone. Mum must have had all these worries in her final years, fretting about who would nurse her when her health deteriorated and who would look after us once she was gone, little knowing she had much less time left than she thought.

I can't describe the overwhelming relief I felt when the results came back and Alex was in the clear. I think I cried more than I did when I'd got my own positive results over two years before. Now I didn't have to worry about him getting ill and we could make concrete plans for his future; I only had to think about myself and how I would deal with the symptoms when they arrived. Honestly, if one of us had to have this horrible disease, I'm happy that it was me rather than Alex. I couldn't have stood nursing him through it if I was in the clear. That would have been too hard.

The other development when Alex turned eighteen was that he bought himself a car with the money he got from Granddad's trust fund. He'd passed the test after his seventeenth birthday. Unfortunately, he hadn't had the car long when he was involved in an accident. It wasn't his fault but his car was a write-off and he couldn't immediately afford a new one. The insurance company said that if he made a claim, he wouldn't be able to get insurance again until he was twenty-one, so he was a bit stuck.

Before he got the car, social services had been paying for him to take taxis to school, at a cost of nearly a thousand pounds a month, but after the accident they refused to fund him any more so it was very hard for him to get to school. Sometimes circumstances just seemed to pile up against us, and I had to keep thinking, 'sink or swim, sink or swim!'

Rather than helping him find a way to get to school more cheaply, they decided he was being rebellious by not going in every day and was therefore not taking his education seriously. No one offered to help him with his university applications, but because I had already been down the same route I knew exactly what he needed to do and we managed without any help from anyone else.

So many times over the years I had promised myself I would never rely on social services for anything, having been let down over and over again. This time, however, I really meant it. I knew that if I waited for them to sort Alex out it would never happen. I was going to have to do it myself, just as I had for my own university applications.

Social services did not believe Alex was going to uni until he was actually there, but he still had to leave the home straight after his last A level exam as he had turned eighteen. Even when he started to get offers of places back from the universities in writing, social services still wouldn't believe that it was actually going to happen. In front of him they said they didn't believe it because he was 'too thick' to go to university. Social services actually wanted to chuck him out into a hostel on the day of his eighteenth birthday, even though he was still in the middle of doing his A levels at the time. I pleaded with them for ages before they eventually agreed to let him stay another week, just to finish the exams, but that was all they were willing to concede. Even if we had still been in foster care the same thing could well have happened because they would have stopped paying for his care the moment he turned eighteen, regardless of whether he was still at school or not. It seemed to me that this was yet another barrier to kids in care getting into further education. How hard would it be to do well in your A levels if you had to move into a hostel half way through the exams?

I was so angry about the injustice of it I wrote to Prime Minister Tony Blair to let him know what was happening. I did get a reply, but it was just to say that he was passing my letter on to the Department for Education and Families. They then wrote to say they couldn't do anything because the law actually states that in the period between leaving school and starting at university a person is officially not in education any more, even though his place has been arranged and all the paperwork has been done. It was a horrific example of a heartless bureaucracy refusing to see what was obviously the right thing to do.

It meant that Alex was not entitled to any accommodation or financial support from social services during the summer between leaving school and starting uni. They wrote to say there wasn't anything they could do because legally Alex wasn't back in education until the first day of his university course. So during those summer holidays I had to find somewhere for both of us to stay. University landlords don't want students hanging around during the holidays and the care home certainly wouldn't have us back now we were both over eighteen. There was nothing else to do but bend the rules if we weren't both going to be spending the summer in my car. I managed to sneak Alex in to stay in my student accommodation, without the landlord knowing, because otherwise he would have been completely homeless throughout the summer. There's no way we could have afforded to rent two rooms.

At the beginning of October 2006 I drove him up to Manchester to start his course, having arranged his accommodation myself and bought all the supplies I knew from my own experience he would need. As far as social services were concerned he had come of age and left the system, so he wasn't their responsibility any longer.

Once he arrived at university he didn't bother to tell anyone about his past history, happy to get on with making new friends and moving forward. He settled in much more quickly and easily than I had, perhaps because he'd had a couple of years on his own in the independent unit before moving out, or maybe just because he has such an easygoing nature.

He started on a computing course in his first year, then moved on to forensics in the second year, learning how to acquire data and maintain its integrity. Working with computers and phones and CCTV cameras is one of the biggest parts of police work these days because the technology contains so many clues and so much information. Someone who knows how to find that information and capture it in a way that it can be used as evidence is a valuable commodity. If Sherlock Holmes were at work today he would almost certainly have these sorts of IT skills as part of his portfolio.

If the police raided a house where they thought some-one had been downloading child pornography, for instance, they would need to call in a professional with Alex's skills to make sure they didn't switch off anything valuable, or make the evidence inadmissible by not following the right procedures. They need to know how to get into a computer's memory while not opening themselves up to accusations of having tampered with it.

Alex was always brilliant with computers, totally confident about them from the day Mum first brought one home for us. He seemed to know instinctively how to put them together and make them work, without having to read any manuals or ask any questions. I was so proud of the way he was taking off in the world on his own and I knew Mum would have been too. Only occasionally did I allow myself to stop and feel sad that she wasn't there to see it.

Chapter Twenty-Three

Alex

When I bought my first car, it felt great to be able to get myself about and be independent, without having to rely on anyone else. Social services agreed to give me just enough petrol money to be able to drive myself to and from school each day, which was a lot less than I had been costing them in taxi fares. But then I had the accident, which messed up everything.

I was in the car with two friends when the one sitting in the front suddenly had an epileptic fit while we were driving along. As I pulled over to draw into a lay-by, my other friend in the back panicked and yanked on the handbrake, which sent the car spinning off the road and into a lamppost, hitting it dead in the centre of the bonnet. It was a complete write-off even though none of us were hurt. I was insured but the insurance company warned that if I made a claim I wouldn't be able to get insurance again until I was twenty-one. We couldn't afford for me not to be driving for another three years so we had to accept that all my inheritance from Granddad had disappeared in those few seconds of skidding across the road.

I was heartbroken about it, and to make matters worse, social services wouldn't go back to paying for taxis for me to get to school, telling me I had to get a bus. Not only did the bus trip take about two and a half hours each way, but the first bus of the day didn't leave early enough to get me to school on time so it became increasingly difficult to get to my lessons. They suggested that I could move schools to be closer to the home, but I was on the verge of taking my A levels and I thought that even with the travel problems it would be better to stay where I was at such a crucial time. I think they actually hoped I would quit school altogether at that stage and take up an apprenticeship somewhere, but all Mum's early brainwashing about the importance of education had sunk too deeply into my subconscious for me to be willing to give up at this late stage. Not that Isobel would have allowed me to anyway.

As usual Isobel went into battle on my behalf, demanding that they help me out with taxi money for a few more months just so that I could get my exams, but even when faced with her full fury they were still adamant. They would pay for the petrol and that was all.

'But he doesn't have a car any more,' Isobel protested down the phone from her university. 'So what good is a petrol allowance?'

'It's your responsibility to make sure he has a car,' they replied. 'All we can do is provide a fuel allowance.'

Luckily for me Isobel had worked as an evening supervisor in a convenience store over the summer and had managed to save a little bit of money so she scraped everything together and bought me an old banger a few weeks later. Although I had missed a good few days at school by that time it was just enough to get me in for the last weeks and I managed to get the A level grades I needed to secure my place at the university I wanted. Yet again Isobel had saved the day simply by refusing to be beaten.

Once I started university and was living in a different town from her, we stopped seeing much of each other during term time, but we still talk every day for at least half an hour, and we always get together in the holidays. We've bought a house together with the money we got from our half of the proceeds from Mum's house, and we've got tenants in and are keeping it as an investment. Needless to say, Isobel arranged all this, just as she's taken care of most of the practical arrangements in our lives since Mum died.

Social services hardly ever get in touch with me now. I think they speak to Isobel from time to time and when she tells them that I'm doing fine, they just say 'Tell him to ring us if he has a problem.' I can't imagine that I ever would now. If I have a problem, I always ring Isobel –

and I hope that she does the same with me. We are so lucky to have each other. I don't think either of us would be where we are today if we had been only children. In fact, I know we wouldn't, because when Mum died and we desperately needed caring adults to look after us, no one listened.

Epilogue

Isobel

By the time I had finished my degree I knew that I wanted to work in children's homes myself. I was sure I could make a real contribution, knowing what I did about the system from the inside. I believe it often lets down the kids in care and want to do as much as I can to right that situation. This is not due to lack of effort by the workers themselves, but because of the way the whole system is set up. I am told that only one per cent of children brought up in care get to university. It has become an accepted fact, even in the care homes themselves, that further education isn't for 'people like us'.

This was brought home to me again when I was working in a care home after I graduated and there was a young girl who was having some troubles. During a conversation with her I assured her I understood how she felt because I had been in care too. I hadn't actually told the staff of the home much about my personal background at that stage, mainly because they hadn't asked, so when word got back to a senior worker she asked me into her office for a chat. She informed me that she had been in the room when the girl mentioned to another member of staff that I had been in care.

'Really?' the staff member had replied. 'But I thought Isobel had been to university.'

This was a woman who worked in the system and had closed her mind to the idea that someone in care could go to university. Yet most children in care are there through no fault of their own, so why don't more of them get a chance of further education? They're not there because they are bad, or stupid, but just because there wasn't anyone willing or able to look after them. Is it simply because society doesn't expect them to go and so does nothing to help them? Apart from the academic work necessary to be accepted by a university, there are also all the administration skills needed to fill out the right forms, get to interviews and organise accommodation. It is hard enough for a young person with two parents and a supportive family to find their way through the maze. What chance is there for someone who is being looked after by social workers who mostly have no expectations for them at all and possibly know nothing about the further education system themselves anyway?

'Actually,' I said, 'the young person is right. I was in care.'

'Ah,' she said knowingly, 'foster care was it?'

It seemed she simply couldn't believe that any child from a unit like the one we were working in could ever get to university.

'No one from this unit has gone on to further education,' she said emphatically.

It's as if some of the people working in the care industry feel defeated by the enormity of the tasks they are confronted with and have closed their minds to the possibility that kids in their care could do well in life. They have no energy or enthusiasm left for helping them to achieve anything beyond the bare minimum. They have no confidence that they can make a difference to the life of any individual child, so they just fulfil their obligations to keep the children safe and go no further than that. Partly it's because they are all so poorly paid. It is hard to recruit enthusiastic, educated and hard-working people and ask them to work incredibly anti-social hours if you are paying virtually nothing. How are they to support their own families?

When I was working in a home myself after I graduated, I found a child who wanted to go to university. I was immediately enthused and wanted to help her get the right forms and fill them in correctly. When I mentioned it to one member of staff she dismissed the idea.

'She's always saying that but it's never going to happen,' was all they said, just as I imagine they must have said to one another about me and Alex when we kept saying we wanted to go into further education.

But why not? Would they give up that easily if it was one of their own children who wanted to improve themselves and learn new things? Should there not be training courses for staff who are in the corporate parenting role to make sure they understand how to fulfil the basic tasks of modern parenthood, such as preparing the children in their care for university? Children in care are supposed to have certain rights, including the right to an education, but few are given the necessary support to claim that right. Because most of them don't know their rights they don't claim them and a lazy system is happy to allow that to happen.

Alex and me both getting to university is actually a huge victory for Mum. All Dad's attempts to undermine her efforts to make us into high achievers have failed. The foundations that she laid for us were strong enough to resist all the negative pressures that Dad's crime unleashed in our lives and I feel proud to think she would not be disappointed in us. Now it is my turn to try to do the same for other kids.

Maybe some good came out of the tragedy that our family went through, in that Alex and I got to see what life was like for children who had no family to care for them, and that insight has given us both a powerful focus for our lives. Seeing first-hand how hard life is for many young people has convinced us that this is an area where we can actually make a real difference.

We have had our eyes opened to just how many people need practical help in other countries as well as the UK. Because our Christmases had been so sad since Mum died, in 2006 Alex and I decided to do something different during the holiday season, rather than trying to emulate some stereotype of a happy family Christmas Day. We realised that if we didn't make a positive plan it would just be the two of us sitting around watching rubbish television together all day. There had to be something else we could do, we reasoned, somewhere we could go where Christmas wasn't so horribly commercialised that anyone who couldn't join in, like us, was made to feel like a complete outsider.

Initially we thought about just booking a holiday that would get us out of the country but when I started looking into it, I found a programme for volunteers to go to Ghana to help educate people about Aids, about basic rules of hygiene and disease prevention, about eating a healthy diet and about the drugs that were available to help. We instantly knew that was how we wanted to spend the holiday – doing something useful and learning something new at the same time.

The village we went to was on an island in the middle of Lake Volta, one of the biggest man-made lakes in the world. It is so big, around 400 kilometres long and 25 kilometres wide, that you can't see the surrounding shore when you're on the island and the fares for crossing it are so high that most of the locals have never even left the island.

Because they are so cut off from the outside world the villagers are consequently missing out on everything, from education to medical supplies. It was touching how grateful they were to us for going to visit them, even though we were so young and the amount of help we could offer was always going to be small. They imagined we lived in a country much better than theirs and they couldn't understand why we would want to go all that way to see them. Despite their obvious poverty, there were many things about their culture that we thought were infinitely superior to what we have in the West.

While we were there we also volunteered in an orphanage on the mainland, interested to see how the system worked in an African country. We threw a Christmas party and put on a play, then invited donations from wealthy audience members to help raise funds so they could move to bigger premises, and we were struck by how different their attitude towards orphans was to anything we had experienced in England. When a child has to go into an orphanage in Ghana the whole village takes responsibility for its care. The government doesn't pay a penny.

no one listened

On another occasion, in the village on the island, a woman who was breast-feeding explained to us that it wasn't her baby.

'If a mother dies while her baby is still small,' she told us, 'another woman will automatically take over the responsibility of breast-feeding it.'

To start with it seemed strange to us that in a community where most people didn't have enough to eat and couldn't afford the medical supplies they needed to survive, there could be so much happiness and generosity of spirit, whereas in England, where everyone has so much, there is a lack of people who want to look after children who have lost their families.

There are charities, of course, that try to fill the gap. I have been working as an independent visitor volunteer for an amazing one called National Youth Advocacy Service (NYAS). The charity assigns me a young person who has been drawn to their attention as someone who might benefit from the scheme. I am given an allowance of fifty pounds a month to take the young person out, which is to cover petrol, food, travel and whatever we might decide to do together. I am expected to take them out for eight hours a month, and I try to do it twice a month for the majority of the day. Sometimes we just go out for a bite to eat or to the cinema, or we might go for a drive or to an amusement park. It gives young people who are looked after by social services a chance to get away from the care system. The role basically involves befriending the child and being there for them as well as taking them out and having fun. It shows them that there is someone else out there who cares about their wellbeing, someone independent of social services who hasn't prejudged them based on their record. It provides them with an escape from where they are living for a few hours. NYAS also has advocacy workers who young people can use to represent their views in meetings and ensure their rights are being met.

There is always a desperate shortage of people in England who want to foster other people's children or work with them in care homes. We have designed our society to function around the nuclear family and when someone falls out of that neat pattern, as we did through no fault of our own, few people have the will to help. There are many dedicated, generous and kind people who work in the care system, but not nearly enough. The best ones are all overworked and underpaid, and consequently unable to do as much good as they might otherwise be able to, and they are often slowed down by bureaucracy and paperwork.

Because young people in care are moved around so often it is much harder for them to develop relationships of trust with the workers. Writing reports and risk assessments means they don't have enough time to provide love and care. Sometimes a young person just needs a hug, which the workers are nervous of giving in case they open themselves up to accusations of having a sexual motive. Many of the workers end up disillusioned because of the system.

In most nuclear families, the parents would never allow their children to change schools so frequently and then to be thrown out into the world at the age of eighteen without any further help and support. Why does society find it acceptable that this should happen to vulnerable young people in the care system? There should be an uproar about this, and changes should be introduced so that kids in care get the same opportunities and support as those growing up with their own families.

Perhaps if the units were smaller, with just a couple of children in each, they would be more like families. There needs to be much more emphasis on education and on continuing to support the young people beyond the ages of sixteen or eighteen, to combat problems like loneliness, drug abuse and homelessness. Everyone is too quick to write off young people in care as 'bad' rather than 'damaged', and to criminalise them too young. We need to establish a system that sets goals for them, gives positive rewards, and is much more supportive of those who choose to continue into further education.

no one listened

It is much easier for the world to forget about inconvenient children like Alex and me. But if children in care received better treatment, all sorts of other problems once they are in the outside world might be avoided.